HOW TO SURVIVE

JOHN HUDSON

HOW TO SURVIVE
SELF-RELIANCE
IN EXTREME
CIRCUMSTANCES

THE COUNTRYMAN PRESS
A Division of W. W. Norton & Company
Independent Publishers Since 1923

For Jen

CONTENTS

If you're going through hell, keep going.

ANON

INTRODUCTION
WHY DO SOME PEOPLE SURVIVE?

On Christmas Eve 1971, a violent thunderstorm raged high above the Peruvian Amazon. Huge black clouds flashed white with lightning over the jungle-covered slopes. Through this churning mass, a small propeller-driven plane was tossed like a scrap of paper in the surging updrafts. LANSA Flight 508, en route from Lima to Pucallpa. Inside the plane, the ninety-two terrified passengers and crew became in turn weightless, then slammed down into their seats, their belongings raining out of the overhead lockers in pitch darkness.

At 12.36 p.m., about halfway into the one-hour journey, all contact with Flight 508 was lost.

Eleven days later, a seventeen-year-old girl crawled out of the jungle. She was the only survivor. Her name was Juliane Koepcke. She would later describe how she saw one of the engines get struck by lightning and the entire plane being ripped apart in mid-air by the violence of the storm.

That Juliane survived falling for two miles without a parachute could be described as miraculous, but the fact she was then able to walk and crawl for ten days through thick jungle with concussion, deep cuts and a broken collarbone, and finally emerge to safety, is at least equally incredible. It sounds like something so extreme as to be beyond under-standing, and certainly beyond what ordinary people are capable of. But Juliane isn't some kind of superwoman, born different from the rest of us. The fact that she survived was down to a sequence of events and behaviours that allowed her to achieve the seemingly impossible but, which when understood and applied correctly, are things we can all do in all of our lives. Let's look at what happened.

The aspect of the story that certainly isn't repeatable, of course, is surviving the fall. When she came to on the forest floor, apart from the broken collarbone, she had cuts, bumps, bruises and eyes swollen half-closed from the force of the impact. No one knows for certain why the fall itself wasn't fatal, but Juliane was seatbelted into a row of three seats which spun around like a sycamore seed as it fell, and she was finally slowed in the last few metres by the branches of the tall trees themselves.

But once she was down in the jungle, there were any number of wrong steps she could have taken. Can you imagine what that must have been like, coming to for the first time, after drifting in and out of consciousness, when your worst fear has come true and you've been sucked out of a plane: a seventeen-year-old, injured, scared, lying on the floor of the jungle as vultures landed in the treetops around her? She had been belted in a seat next to her mother, but there was no sign of her now. After she had managed to stand and after searching for her mother for an entire day with no success, she had to decide what to do. The first thing she had to do was overcome the very human impulse to give up before she began. What would you do first? Try and find other survivors? Look for food and water? Tend your wounds as best you could? Look for things you could use from the wreckage of the plane? Make a shelter? The normal advice in any survival situation is to stay at the site of the incident if you can. If Juliane had stayed put in the forest and waited to be rescued she'd still be there today, absorbed into the jungle soil beneath her seat like the others.

Juliane, however, had something absolutely invaluable. Knowledge. She had spent two years being home-schooled in the Amazon jungle by her parents, who were both research scientists. She knew that this was an environment that she could survive in.

Critically, she also knew that the jungle canopy was too thick for rescuers to see her where she was lying, and that she had no means to signal to them. She had to move. But where? The jungle stretched in every direction, it hummed and seethed with all sorts of life, much of it, she knew, potentially dangerous. So she thought back to the advice that her father had given her about getting rescued in dense tropical forest. She sat up and listened. And that's when she heard the sound of trickling water. She remembered his tip that following water would lead you to people. So that's what she did. Hardly able to see anything without her glasses and with only one shoe, she limped and crawled along the stream, which eventually became a river, for over 200 hours. She had to put her one-shoed foot tentatively forwards each time to avoid the jungle's many thorns and fangs. The only food she had was a single bag of sweets she'd found after the crash. The temptation to give in must have been enormous, but she kept going, dragging herself along, one metre at a time. After a week or so one of her wounds became infested with maggots, but she kept going and was eventually able to get them out by dousing them in petrol she found in a hut used by loggers. Ultimately, it was those workers who found her, semi-conscious in their hut, and were able to take her on the ten-hour boat trip to the nearest village. In the years afterwards, Juliane became a biologist, specializing in Peruvian bats and working in a zoological library in Munich. In 2010, she published a memoir. In an interview around publication, she said, 'I had nightmares for a long time, for years, and of course the grief about my mother's death and that of the other people came back again and again. The thought "Why was I the only survivor?" haunts me. It always will.'[1]

The question of why she survived haunted Juliane, it was a kind of guilt. But later it was reported that fourteen other passengers survived the fall to the jungle floor, strewn widely over a massive area, but didn't make it out.* So the question takes on another more literal quality for me: why her? What was different about her?

What she was able to do, after the initial luck that gave her the opportunity, was to prioritize, utilize specific knowledge and fundamental principles and apply them to her situation in a flexible way. She didn't freeze, she remembered one piece of crucial advice, prioritized correctly, was adaptable, and then didn't let anything stop her, task by task, inch by inch, in spite of every mental and physical hurdle put in front of her.

What she did was remarkable, but not unrepeatable.

In this book, I want to introduce you to people like Juliane, partly because their incredible stories offer inspiration but also because the way that they approached their situations can teach us so much about how we deal with decisions in our own lives.

Because one thing I know is that bad things happen. Some people deal with them. Some don't. Hopefully very few of us will ever find ourselves in the exact situations described in the book, but we can all learn life skills from them.

By studying the choices people have made under the most extreme pressure, where the stakes are highest, we can learn how it's possible to teach our brains to make better choices whenever we have to make them.

* Though this is a topic of some debate.

Why have I written this book?

My day job is Chief Survival Instructor to the UK military. What that means is that I train the instructors, who in turn teach every serviceman and woman in the British military how to survive. I spend my time travelling the world, seeking out the newest ideas and technologies and how they might be applied in some of the most extreme environments known to humanity. I've trekked through the world's driest deserts and its most remote jungles. I've been dumped into freezing water, trudged across barren tundra and been hunted through forests.

Right now, I'm writing this introduction in the closest thing to a moon base that I can think of; I'm nearer to the North Pole than to a tree. The sun will come back above our white horizon in this part of the Arctic next week. We made headlines a while ago when the temperatures here were lower than those on Mars.

It feels like another world too. The snow sounds different when you move on it; it's frozen hard and squeaks just like polystyrene as you take a step. The freezing air even feels different in my nostrils as I breathe it in, the little hairs freeze rigid as the air passes them, making my nose feel sticky inside. I've left my snow machine running outside, its headlights forming a pool of yellow in the cool blue twilight of midday; engines are hard to start when it's really cold so it's better and safer not to turn them off once they're going.

When reaching for a door's metal handle up here, I leave my gloves on even though it's warm on the other side, centimetres away. Touching metal at these temperatures with bare skin can cause frostbite – flash-freezing your flesh. The door is unlocked like all the others round here; you don't want to have to fumble through many layers of warm clothing for keys if you're being followed by a hungry polar bear. Here, being absent-minded can get you killed quickly; prioritization isn't an optional extra.

I've spent years communicating that to people of all sorts of abilities from all sorts of different backgrounds and listening to how different their approach to problem solving is to mine. I've also done my fair share of sitting in offices too – as you can imagine, there's a lot of admin and reports that go along with the exciting stuff – and I have come to apply survival principles in my everyday life. I know from what others tell me that they find the techniques useful in their lives too, especially their working lives.

Over the last twenty years I've also been collecting survival stories and attempting to essentialize what survival is and how we do it. A great truism is that a wise person learns from their mistakes; a wiser one learns from the mistakes of others. When I train survival instructors I like to include stories of past survivors, alongside examples of those that weren't so lucky.

Although our culture is full of disaster and survival stories, from Homer's *Odyssey*, to *Robinson Crusoe*, to *Titanic*,* we rarely properly analyse why some people survive and some don't.† We either ascribe it to blind luck, or to something more innate. The real answer is that we can all be better at developing the sort of mindset that allows us to make better decisions under pressure. Of course, the very best training for dealing with a situation is having experienced it first hand before, but there are a multitude of easier things we can all do to be better prepared.

That's where my team come in. The practical world of military survival is all about learning a single, simple template that can be transposed anytime, anywhere. The people we train have enough going on in their heads with their day jobs, so survival rules have to be simple, memorable and multi-purpose. It's about working out what's important and what isn't, what's going to hurt you first and what you can do to give yourself the best chance of success. Once we understand our bodies' physical necessities – from their normal baseline 'tick-over' to the very edges of their performance capabilities – we can truly know our own limits. And once we know those boundaries, we can work out strategies to surpass them, by how we approach the situation in front of us. For best results our actions need to be done in the

* One piece of advice I'd definitely have given Jack was that there was easily enough room for them both on the bit of wood.
† Most people these days think survival mainly involves eating ever more disgusting things (because this makes good TV). It doesn't.

right sequence, and this doesn't mean memorizing abstract checklists – I hate them. The key is appreciating how the human body, and most importantly, the mind functions, and using that understanding to increase your performance under pressure.

Your most important tool

I get asked a lot what the best tool to carry for survival is. It's not a fancy knife, or a geo-location device. The most important tool you can have with you for survival – or any kind of situation requiring self-reliance – is a well-stocked brain. Unfortunately, unlike most survival gear, it doesn't come with a user manual and subsequently many of us aren't using ours in the best way.

More than ever today, we find ourselves barraged with information, with demands on our attention, which all seem equally loud, equally urgent. Many people spend their lives frantically checking their emails, cycling from one app on their smartphone to the next, refreshing their devices but not themselves. This information barrage means that we get the same sense of having solved a problem by making that little unread messages number on our phone disappear, or by posting on social media, as from solving a real problem in our lives, and the reward is much more immediate. This 'problem solving' fires the same circuits in our brain, gives that same little hit of pleasurable dopamine as true problem solving, but it's constant and it's exhausting us. At the same time, we never have to remember a phone number, or use a map – we can find out almost anything without having to remember it and our attention spans are shot to pieces. It's like we're only training one muscle in the gym and leaving everything else to wither away. We're out of balance.

Now, I'm no Luddite, I use technology all the time, but we're carrying all this extra equipment that we think is essential – it isn't – and we're constantly weighed down by it. We've stopped solving actual problems for ourselves, so when a problem occurs, we don't know how to go back to first principles. What survival teaches us is to essentialize, to carry only what we need. When we travel lighter, we travel faster and cover greater distances.

I've trained individuals who've suffered traumatic experiences on survival courses. I've seen first hand the confidence that comes from realizing they are equipped to deal with anything that can be thrown at them. I want to put all of that knowledge into this book. If I can give you one tiny part of the freedom and self-reliance that I know comes from realizing you can be dropped into pretty much any situation and be OK, then I'll have succeeded.

We can all survive better

This book isn't a traditional 'survival manual' though.* In all likelihood, you won't ever need to use the knowledge in this book in a life-threatening situation, which is a good thing. The real advantage to military survival skills is that because they are a set of guiding principles, their ethos can be applied to any situation.

We are all forced to make choices constantly, to try and deal with setbacks, to react to shocking news, to prioritize tasks and face things that seem insurmountable. We will likely all face moments when our spirit is tested. The stories of survivors and how they accomplished what they did are a treasure trove of information on how we can approach these moments of crisis.

Because the fact is, whether it's a shipwreck in the eighteenth century or a text message that changes your world for ever, humans all have the same type of brain with which to process everything, and the way we respond to new situations hasn't really caught up with how vastly different life is for most of us in the developed world. Luckily, it also turns out that what we do when we're dealing with the unexpected – when we're under pressure, when the stakes are so high that the unimportant things fall away – is focus

* Though you probably will pick up some survival tips along the way.

on those essential things that keep us motivated and help us to achieve, and that ultimately make us happy.

In my world, if you make the fire right, it lights, if you construct a shelter correctly, you stay dry. As a species, we are innately drawn to this sort of thing; after all, the sorts of things we do when we apply survival thinking are the things we've been doing as a species for most of our existence, so it's no wonder we're set up to find them pleasurable. If applying the lessons in this book brings a tiny bit of these goal-directed rewards back into everyday life, I'll have done my job.

But more than this, I think there are, on a far broader level, many lessons from the world of extreme survival which are clearly applicable to anyone. For example, one of the most popular misconceptions about extreme events is that some people just naturally or instinctively know what to do, or how to survive, in any situation – while others don't and never will. Time after time, we see the hero act while everyone else panics or freezes; the myth gets repeated, instilling in the rest of us a 'why bother even trying' mindset when confronted with *seemingly* impossible tasks.

But I can tell you, categorically, there is no mysterious singular 'Will to Survive' or survival gene that some people have while others don't. Of course, some people bring different levels of handy skills, or others have relevant experiences that can give them a little head start in a new challenge.

But while we may not all get gold medals in the race, we could all cross the finish line.

Survival reminds us that if something is difficult then we have two choices; try harder or stop trying. Stopping trying in survival normally means dying.

Survival often comes down to your ability to keep putting in effort even when you're feeling discomfort. When it's getting dark and you're soaking wet and you have to get over the next ridge before you can make a shelter, you quickly realize the universe doesn't owe you anything. The survival mindset has no room for entitlement.

The lessons from survival training involve working hard and accepting temporary hardship; but they lead to an increased ability to deal with whatever life can throw at you.

Working at the edge of human experience reminds us again and again that becoming competent at anything new takes concentration and effort. These are crucial things that I believe it is worth reminding every leader, employee, colleague and parent of.

We'll start by looking at the distillation of every successful survival story I've studied.

The Survival Triangle

Below is the Survival Triangle, my personal unpicking of how people cope in the direst circumstances, the essence of this book.

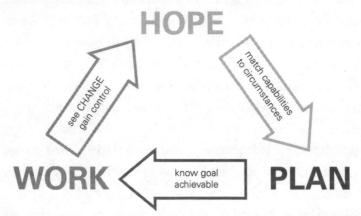

Pared down to its simplest form, the Survival Triangle essentially states: 'If I can do anything to change my situation, I will begin to feel in control of it; if I feel in control of my situation then I can sustain hope; with hope I can form a plan; with a plan my efforts are directed most efficiently to my goals.' The Survival Triangle, in combination with a few practical skills, gives you a pre-made planning template which can be used to jumpstart the whole survival process.

Through my research into historical cases, I've found that if one of the three corners of the triangle is missing, then survival is unlikely. If two are missing, it's almost impossible. As a caveat, the only thing I know of that can replace one of the Survival Triangle's corners is luck. Luck, however, is a factor that is beyond our control; expecting it is a risky strategy.*

Over the following pages, we'll look at the importance of effort, hope and goals and the factors that contribute to them, so that you can form a self-sustaining survival process, your own perseverance feedback loop. Over the years I've learned that hope in survival situations is the result of realistic optimism, generated by matching my capabilities to my circumstances. And to tackle any problem effectively I need a plan. My ultimate target of success is most easily attained via a plan with a series of smaller goals as waypoints en route. Once I know that my next small goal is achievable, I can start to work at reaching it. Work is, simply, directed, efficient effort that will eventually change my situation – I therefore gain control of it. If I can control my situation, I can sustain my hope. And repeat.

I've applied this Survival Triangle – my perseverance feedback loop – when I've been in many extreme environments and situations, and it's always worked for me. But you don't need to be trudging alone through tundra to use this simple method. You can practice by applying it to any task that, at first glance, creates a gut reaction which

---

* As one of my colleagues was once told in his annual report, 'Luck is an enviable quality in any aviator, but it is unwise to rely on it so heavily, so early in one's career.'

tells you it's too much. Most of us would react with horror to the news that we have been chosen to write an important ninety-page report, due in a month. We'd probably stick it on the bottom of our to-do list and ignore it guilt-ily until we had two weeks left, then one. But if we plan properly and prioritize this report, break it down into writing three pages a day, we're much more likely to start. Then it's about making sure you do write three pages a day with focused effort. As you get each three-page chunk in the bag, you'll get the satisfaction of progress each day, of controlling your situation. Flooded with realistic opti-mism, you'll drive onwards with a far greater chance of executing your plan.

Everything in this book is essentially about giving you the tools to make the Survival Triangle function more effec-tively in your life. Don't worry if it feels too abstract right now, we'll keep coming back to it until it's second nature.

I've structured the book so that the first two chapters are about preparation and planning, Chapter 3 is about how we can best approach getting things done – what I call 'Work' in the triangle – and Chapter 4 is about how we sustain hope, our perseverance engine.

Chapters 5 and 6 are about how to best make use of the people and information around us to inform all three sides of the triangle, and Chapters 7 and 8 are about bringing it all together as we move through life.

First things first

I've learned that the best way to use your brain to maximum advantage is to know its capabilities first, take a short tour of its features, a bit like the pre-flight walk-round check a pilot makes. Knowing how we behave helps us to make the most of our current circumstances, which warning signs to look out for, and the most advantageous ways to deal with problems before they spiral out of control.

The unexpected

The foundation underlying all the survival training that I deliver is an understanding of how we initially respond to any bad situation. These theories were developed to show how we react in disastrous situations, but you can apply them to almost any stressful event. The textbook model was identified by survival psychologist John Leach after years of studying survivors – and the actions of those who weren't so fortunate. John is a rare type of psychologist; a specialist in human behaviour during extreme circumstances, and also an RAF-trained and -qualified survival instructor. The model he has described covers the things that we humans normally do when there's any threat to our life. His explanation of survivor behaviour is borne out by both extensive research and personal experience. The model has five parts, and it describes the normal arc of any event by breaking it into key stages – Pre-Impact, Impact, Recoil, Rescue and Post-Traumatic – each with their own typical behaviour patterns.[2] At points in this book, I'll refer to these stages, as it's important to keep in mind that the vast majority of us will tend to be stunned by shocking new events that we have absolutely no frame of reference for, but that we can all adapt afterwards. It helps us to better deal with our actions later if we know that the way we initially behaved is normal for our species. Even better, knowing this and thinking ahead can really help us to react positively should we face adversity in our lives.

So let's start by taking a look at how our brains deal with unexpected events and just how important the right sort of planning is.

Chapter 1

PREPARING TO FAIL

Dale Zelko looked down over his right shoulder through the cockpit window and saw the dark sky suddenly flare as two surface-to-air missiles tore up towards him through the low cloud over Belgrade.

This wasn't supposed to happen.

Dale was a US Air Force fighter pilot sitting in an F-117 Nighthawk stealth fighter – the black angular ones that look like a UFO – a jet that was considered by most people at the time to be pretty much invulnerable. Dale's aircraft was called a stealth fighter because it was 'low-observable', but that doesn't mean it was invisible. It was black and flew at night, it was angular in shape to make radar waves bounce off in ways that are harder to detect, its jet engines were deep inside and their exhausts were shrouded to dissipate noise and heat. Its bombs were carried inside its fuselage to stop them reflecting radar waves. Even the jet's black paint was specially mixed to absorb radar energy and reduce its on-screen signature. Hundreds of billions of dollars of cutting-edge science had gone into making sure that no stealth fighter had ever been shot down by an enemy.

And yet at that moment, as he watched the missiles arc upwards, Dale realized that his jet was about to have the dubious distinction of being the first.

The missiles weighed a ton each, were six metres long, with a bright orange flame spewing grey smoke, travelling at three times the speed of sound. The first one flew straight over the top of him, close enough that its shockwave buffeted his jet. He remembers being surprised that it didn't go off – surface-to-air missiles like those are fitted with a proximity fuse that detonates their 60 kg explosive warhead when they get close to their targets, peppering them with small shards of metal shrapnel. He looked back, saw the next one and thought, *It's going to run right into me.*

The force of the impact was so violent that Dale's jet flipped over and its nose pitched down simultaneously, throwing him up in his seat straps so that he was pushing up against the cockpit roof and enduring an incredible negative g-force of 7; seven times the force of gravity, in the wrong direction. As his aircraft dived out of his control, he needed to pull the ejection-seat handle that would rocket him out of it within the next couple of seconds, if he didn't want to spear into the ground at 500 mph.

In life, we all have to deal with unexpected events. Not

many of us will find ourselves fired out of a jet thousands of feet above the Earth, but in our professional and personal lives, it will often be how we respond to the unexpected that will most define us. However, perfectly understandably, most people spend very little time thinking about failure, disaster and worst-case scenarios. Indeed, the unexpected is by definition the thing you haven't planned for. We see this time and time again in the most extreme of circumstances. While we can't predict what events we'll find ourselves in – be they natural disasters like earthquakes, or man-made catastrophes like violent attacks – what we do know is that our human behaviour in difficult situations tends to follow distinct patterns. These patterns always occur, and they have been observed in studies when random groups of people are subjected to the same stressors.[3] Analyses of these studies reveal not only what proportion of us are likely to respond appropriately – by which I mean doing something to aid survival – during the heat of a 'disaster', and therefore live to tell the tale, but also what the hazards or barriers are to 'coping' after the dust has settled.

Roughly speaking, we all fall into one of three groups during a dynamic crisis event. A few people will know what to do (roughly one in ten), the vast majority of us will not know what to do – we'll be stunned – and a minority of people will react badly. Whether you're in the top, middle or bottom group, we are all liable to behave in those ways unless we retrain ourselves.[4] But this retraining isn't the mammoth task you might think.

By looking at the ways in which Dale Zelko's preparation and mindset allowed him to react appropriately to this most unexpected of events, we can understand how we all have the capacity to cope better, and gain insight into the simple things that we can do to improve how we respond.

The first thing to keep in mind is that new responses are much slower to present themselves than ones we've already prepared.* The second is that we don't make the best decisions when we feel under threat. We all intuitively know that to be true, but let's have a quick look at why that is.

Our brains have been developing for about seven million years, with the majority of that growth squeezed into the last two million. We know from DNA analysis that all of us alive today share a common ancestor from as recently as 190,000 years ago. We come from 'Mitochondrial Eve' or 'Y-Chromosome Adam' and we all have big brains running the same old software. We also know from skull records that when our species, *Homo sapiens*, first appeared on the plains of Africa around 200,000 years ago, its brain was about the same size as ours are now. In other words, we haven't had a hardware update in 200,000 years.†

---

* Anyone who's ever sat through a groom's speech at a wedding where they thought they'd 'wing it' knows this.
† A human fossil recently discovered in Morocco, dated to 300,000 years old, puts the emergence of our species even further back, and was found among flint tools and fire remnants.

Perfectly logically, the oldest bits of the brain are the ones that deal with movement, heart rate, temperature regulation and other fundamentals – this is often called the 'lizard brain', as these are the functions we share with a vast range of species, including lizards. Next, us mammals evolved to have the limbic brain, which is the seat of memories. It stores things we've experienced that were agreeable and disagreeable, and is therefore key to our emotional responses. The final bit to develop was the neocortex, which is where all of the bits that make us human kick in – language, abstract thought, planning, consciousness and imagination. In reality, all of these different bits are very strongly linked and all work together, but as a useful rough outline for our purposes it's important to keep in mind this basic structure.

In his book *Thinking Fast and Slow*, the psychologist Daniel Kahneman characterized the way we think into two distinct systems: the 'slow system' is the rational brain, which is effectively responsible for all the neocortex-related heavy lifting – responding to new situations, problem solving, future planning; and the 'fast system', which takes care of pretty much everything else. The fast system is the reason you don't need to consciously think of every individual step you take to start the car and pull away. It's become routine, and therefore doesn't use up bandwidth in the slow part of your brain.

If you've ever had that experience of fleetingly thinking a bathrobe left on a chair in a dark room is an intruder, and feeling your stomach do that thing it does as fear washes over you – before your conscious brain engages and you rationalize – then you'll have felt how much quicker the older parts of our brain are at reacting to a potential threat than the newer bits. Ancestors who had to consciously think, *Ah, an intruder in the camp, I wonder what their motives are*, wouldn't have lasted long.

It's also worth keeping in mind that it's not just your brain that is affected. The nerves that radiate out from your spinal cord go all over your body, transmitting information about you and the world around you to and from your brain and organs. When we are in dangerous situations, like being too close to a predator (or a bathrobe that looks like one), part of this network, the catchily titled 'sympathetic autonomic nervous system', kicks in.

You've probably heard of it before as the 'fight, flight or freeze' reaction. It prepares your body for immediate action by dilating your pupils to capture more information visually, and dilating the bronchia in your lungs, which increases your intake of oxygen. It accelerates your heart rate to push more oxygen-rich blood to your muscles, makes you sweat to prevent overheating, and ups the secretion of adrenaline. It also stops your body wasting energy on functions that won't be needed in an emergency – it inhibits digestion, reduces saliva production, and stops other 'secondary' muscle functions, notably in the bladder and bowels.

It's also the reason behind the dry mouth and butterflies that you feel when you're confronting something stressful, like a job interview or giving an important presentation. We only have one set of biological processes to deal with stress and they evolved to deal with short, sharp moments of crisis before fading out when we move to safety. Unfortunately, in today's world, we are often receiving tiny bursts of constant stress, whether they're from the tyranny of the email inbox on our smartphone or rolling news. It's also important to keep in mind that the fast system can be pretty unreliable. Much in the same way that the intruder isn't there, often a perceived threat isn't real. That email from a colleague might be passive–aggressive or it might just be the equivalent of a bathrobe over a chair. Many of us now live in a wash of constant low-level stress, which is bad for our bodies but also bad for our ability to make good decisions.

At its most debilitating, this can lead to something known as panic disorder, in which sufferers have unexpected attacks of panic and fear in their everyday lives.

It's important to understand what this real panic is. The portrayal of 'survival situations' in film and media could make you think that panic is the default response of most people, that if something bad happens that's what we'll all do. Well, thankfully it's not, but it does make for dramatic scenes on screen, so we tend to see it there quite frequently.

Panic is the kind of response that has actually lingered in our cultural subconsciousness for thousands of years. It's named after the Greek god Pan, a chaotic maker of mischief who – legend has it – chases us through dark or forbidding places. The legend of Pan has been repeated down the millennia because anything with a strong emotional aspect to it, like panic – or what we might confront in those dark places – tends to be more memorable; more fascinating.

Thankfully, true panic is actually very rare, and it only occurs when certain key ingredients, or factors, are present. The only time I've ever witnessed genuine panic in a survival scenario was when I first did the 'dunker' as a pilot. I was in a very small module in the UK military's helicopter underwater escape trainer. Me and my friend were numbers five and six on the back row of seating in the sealed metal tube, and numbers one to four were pretty much non-swimmers. Now that's a recipe for proper panic. When you're strapped into a metal box that's being submerged; and people can't swim; and the windows are all shut; and the water's rising; then you witness true panic. As the water got higher and the air pocket got smaller it was like being in a washing machine with blindfolded karate experts, all flailing arms and legs. A panic response in humans is usually triggered by these sorts of rare key factors combining: normally a perceived restriction in available *space* and/or *time*, like you could get in a sinking ship or smoke-filled building.

What we almost always mean when we talk about panic as it relates to more everyday anxiety is that feeling of tightness in the chest and the heart beating too fast. If you ever feel the symptoms of 'panic' welling up in your chest during your day-to-day stuff – maybe a tight deadline is making you feel really anxious at the expense of getting your task done – try putting your free hand on the top of your stomach just below your ribs. Close your eyes to concentrate and close your mouth so that you're only breathing through your nose. As you breathe in, feel your stomach area expand under your hand. Try to breathe in and out slowly to a count of four; four in, four out, feeling your stomach rise and fall. This slow, deep breathing rebalances the amounts of oxygen and carbon dioxide in your blood and disengages our primitive fight or flight response. A calm, even breathing rhythm is the key and it can take a few minutes to achieve, but you should find that your heart rate gets back to normal and you start to feel better. Once you get good at it you can try 'triangular breathing', where you hold the inhale for another count of four before you exhale. Try triangular breathing lying down if you find it hard to get to sleep.

What you're doing is tricking your brain into engaging the opposite response to the fight, flight or freeze one (the sympathetic autonomic nervous system). The opposite response you want to switch on, the para-sympathetic autonomic nervous system, is best known as the 'Rest and Digest' response. So the slow and steady breathing gradually puts the influential chemicals in your system back into a calmer balance.

Breathing techniques like this are brilliant because they can be applied pretty much anywhere, in situations from disasters to public speaking. Another great technique for hacking into the Rest and Digest response is to chew gum. Research by survival psychologist Sarita Robinson has found that chewing can engage the Rest and Digest response, lowering your stress-chemical levels and un-fogging your brain.[5] It's one I've instinctively employed for years, like when I'm driving in heavy traffic or late at night, and now there's some survival world research to back it up too.

What this means is that, if we want to make better decisions, we need to try and do two things: 1) try and make as much room in our rational brain as possible and 2) try and reprogram the brain out of the wrong shortcuts it takes when it feels under threat from a new situation.

As we'll see throughout this book, whatever you can do to try and gather information, work out what's happening and take yourself out of this 'under threat' mode will allow you to re-engage your rational, slow brain.

The importance of rewards

The other incredibly important thing to keep in mind is that your brain has a whole other set of very important circuits that, rather than responding to threats and trying to avoid things that make us feel bad, reward us for doing certain things by giving us pleasure. There are lots of things that we do, from food and sex to novel experiences, that result in a little hit of dopamine. The one that will keep coming up throughout this book is how our brains respond to successful problem solving. Simply put: our brains love solving problems, finding out new things and feeling like we're a valued part of the group. What you'll see again and again is that those who survive are able to turn a situation that begins as a threat around through useful actions, which also trigger small rewards from the brain in the midst of the survival situation.

Learn to drill

Whenever your body is working in under-threat mode, your adrenal glands also release the stress hormone cortisol to temporarily increase energy production. One of cortisol's other effects is to inhibit the laying down of new memories by your brain's hippocampus, which explains why even though he must have done so, Dale Zelko has no memory of pulling the emergency eject handle in his stricken stealth fighter.*

No matter how hard he tries, his memory of it is missing, yet it happened. The next thing he remembers is sitting in

---

* Your memory creation is similarly inhibited if your blood alcohol concentration (BAC) gets above 0.2 per cent, hence the patchy plotlines of any really boozy night out.

the ejection seat, watching his cockpit recede into the night below him, the many warning lights blinking in reds and yellows. That he was able to do all this so instinctively when it mattered is because he had repeatedly drilled what to do in the event of emergency, both back on the ground and importantly *in his head*, until it didn't involve producing a new response on race day.

This is why all military aircrews get specialist training for worst-case scenarios, aka 'survival training', whether they like it or not – because, one day, that training cheque may need to be cashed in. And when that day comes, you really don't want to be relying on the slow parts of your brain to come up with every response. So we survival instructors drag our students behind boats at sea in their parachute harnesses, to simulate being blown along after ejection over water, and to practise the drills needed to avoid drowning. We drop them off by helicopter in the dead of night and have them hunted by tracker teams, to practise the skills needed to avoid capture in hostile territory. Any type of training is easiest to remember if it's recent but, when push comes to shove, the very fact that you've done some training, even if it was a long time ago, can pay off. We remember actions much better if we've physically done them – rather than just thought, heard or read about them – and the more times we practise the actions, the more deeply they get ingrained in our brains.

Hard evidence of this phenomenon has been found by

scientists who carried out comparative brain scans of London taxi drivers studying for their infamous navigational test: 'The Knowledge'. In that training, the would-be taxi drivers have to learn to orientate themselves through 25,000 London locations by memory alone; no satnavs allowed. The scans found that the brains of taxi drivers who had gained that knowledge – via four years of study and road training – had significantly grown the areas of their brain associated with memory; the hippocampus. Through learning the many streets of London, they'd taken their mind muscles to the gym and got bigger brains as a result. Similar results have recently been obtained when the brains of 'memory athletes' were scanned at rest and during a test that involved trying to memorize seventy-two random words.[6] These scans showed increased interconnectivity between regions of the brain, showing that having a better memory can be learned. We can change our brains if we want to.

Passing The Knowledge is an extreme end of this spectrum, but as with all things that need to be recalled and actioned quickly, mental rehearsal helps and practise makes perfect. As part of the same learning process, and well before any survival-specific environmental training takes place, military aircrew like Dale Zelko are trained in how to deal with aircraft emergencies. On-board emergencies come in all shapes and sizes, and how to respond to them is learned by heart. Much like the survival drills we'll look at later, aircraft emergency drills are conducted in a very specific sequence and there is no ambiguity about content or order. That's because we don't want to have to think about it – we practise it again and again on the ground until it's second nature in the air. Baby Royal Air Force pilots even get 'cardboard cockpits' so that they can practise their emergency drills back at their pit during downtime.* These mock-ups are printed out life-size, to enable muscle movements and hand gestures to be repeated as 'touch-drills' until they become instinctive.

Just in case the trainee pilot is flying solo and blanks when the emergency happens, all of the 'what-to-do' information is immediately available in their Flight Reference Cards. These cards are a simple, two-sided flip-book of essential drills, which are designed to fit in their flying suit pocket and be carried at all times. To make the emergency stuff easy to find, it occupies one side of each reference card and is coloured bright red. This system is so effective that other branches of the armed forces have adopted it – the ones used by soldiers for ground emergencies are called 'flap sheets'.†

---

* Pit – *n*. RAF Trainee Pilot's smelly sweat-pit of a bedroom in the aptly named Officers' Mess.
† There's no one-size-fits-all policy for all businesses, but for my money, you should have the equivalent of flap sheets for key processes at work. If all you have is a 132-page 'how to do everything at work' Word document buried somewhere on the mythical shared drive, it's basically unusable information, and you've over-complicated things.

Pilot emergency drills are really just like a longer, more involved version of learning to do an emergency stop in a car; something everyone gets asked to do on their driving test, for a very good reason. How to perform a rapid stop, without skidding or stalling, is not the kind of thing that you want to be working out for yourself the first time that someone steps into the street in front of your vehicle. The movement of your foot from the accelerator to the brake pedal becomes quicker and surer the more times you practise this action, making it instinctive. Drivers are not allowed out onto the roads until they master it. It's all done in a pre-drilled sequence because, as we've seen, it's hard to create novel behaviours when your adrenal glands have just dumped lots of stress hormones into your system.

For Dale, this involved drilling himself until ejecting became a reflex. Now we can't prepare exactly as he did (there is no ejector seat handle in most of our lives) but the fundamental principle is the same. We might not be able to prepare *exactly* for the sorts of unexpected situations we'll experience in everyday life, but to make better decisions we need to have pre-loaded our system with comparable ideas *before* our equivalent of seeing the flash, feeling the earth shake, hearing the bang, or smelling the smoke.

What now?

A very simple thing you can do to improve how you might respond under pressure is to think about the sorts of things that might throw a spanner in the works in a given scenario. If you're on your way to make a crucial presentation, think about what the worst question you could be asked might be. What if your laptop won't connect to the screen? What if the train is cancelled, the motorway is solid with traffic? Don't just think about how awful those things would be – plan how you would respond to them.

Imagine your next encounter with your boss. Pre-think the difficult question that they are most likely to ask you when they probe whatever task you're dealing with for them. You probably know them well enough to gauge what their motivations are in doing this. They will have an opinion about your answer to their question, which tends to be expressed as another question, so have the answers to that pre-prepared too. If you can come up with solid reasons to the next thing they'll ask, by 'what if . . .' thinking that too, you won't get caught on the hop. Answering it all with confidence is half the battle, and you gain that by not being surprised into freezing.

Once again, this doesn't mean simply thinking over and over again *Oh no, what if it all goes wrong?* Think of specific scenarios, with specific responses. Get it down on paper. The simplest way you can free up more space for the new thoughts you need to have is to outsource those you can to paper. Make your own flap sheet. If it's in your head, it's taking up space. Draw a diagram of your role in a project with five or so essential parts to it. What do you do if any one of them goes wrong? Try adding a variety of responses and imagining how they might play out. By increasing the number of scenarios you think about, maths dictates that the amount of truly unexpected events gets smaller. Unless you work somewhere where you're reinventing the wheel every time, you'll build up a basic store of scenarios and responses without them needing to have actually happened. This will never replace the value of first-hand experience, but by taking steps to disaster-proof the future, you're actually decreasing the chance of disaster. In fact, you're reframing things entirely, so that it's just an alternate scenario.

Visualizing success is all very well and good and should certainly be part of what we do, but it's only by imagining the unexpected that we begin the process of responding more quickly and decisively should it occur. What you'll hopefully find is that, paradoxically, this is actually a wholly positive process. By pre-equipping yourself with potential solutions to potentially difficult scenarios, you increase the number of positive outcomes.

How to equip your ejector seat

Something I'm frequently asked to do is advise on what to put into military aircraft survival packs and pouches; I'm writing this chapter after returning from doing just that at an ejection seat factory. These are always interesting design challenges, because in some aircraft the entire survival kit contents need to be shoehorned into a space the size of an A4 box file underneath the cushion of a pilot's seat. That's all the room there is to put in whatever is needed to not die in the Arctic or desert or jungle.

There are some guiding principles for this task. Ideally everything should be compact and have multiple uses – why carry lots of heavy stuff when one thing could do many jobs? – a Swiss Army knife approach. So a foil survival blanket will keep you warm, be a tarp shelter to keep you dry, be a reflective surface to signal for rescue, catch rainwater to drink etc., etc. I also try to avoid single points of failure; if I ensure many items overlap on the same key tasks I avoid the problem of one item's loss causing the ultimate failure of the whole system. For example, more than one thing in the pack should be able to signal for rescue – by day or night – and they shouldn't all rely on electrical power, because batteries have a habit of running out. Avoiding redundancy in the system is critical, failure to do so is why we see so many examples of people who rely on one critical item, and when it fails they get lost and have to be rescued. The latest culprit is the smartphone, whose amazing array of useful functions is a huge asset to any trip, until the battery or screen dies. That's when the alternative device or skill should be on hand to assist, but all too often isn't.

For tasks like navigating in unfamiliar, remote zones, I always have several options to help guide me, not just one fragile smartphone. In military survival we list this under the handy mnemonic 'PACE'; Primary, Alternate, Contingency and Emergency. So, to navigate, my primary means are my Ordnance Survey map and Silva compass, my alternate is my pocket GPS, my contingency could be a smartphone and for emergency I carry a magnetized needle to point north, and I know how to navigate using the many signs in nature.

Try getting into the habit of using PACE in your life, to give yourself multiple ways of solving a situation. So let's say you're heading to that job interview – try and make sure you have multiple ways of getting there, so that if the car won't start, or traffic isn't moving, you aren't starting from scratch. You probably won't always need all four, three might do it, but just the process of running the possible scenarios and listing responses will mean you pre-plan more fully. Which means you'll feel more prepared overall.

After the bang

Pulling the handle of his bang-seat – only 1.4 seconds ago –
was just the first step on Dale's new journey. Although it
was late at night and poor weather, the light from the
almost-full moon allowed Dale to see that he had perhaps a
few minutes before he would land in enemy territory, so he
took a moment to consider his options. He had the mental
capacity to do this while hanging in his parachute harness
because of all the time and thought he'd put in before the
flight, mentally going through his 'what if . . .' scenarios. If
he hadn't routinely thought ahead about exactly this kind of
nightmare and worked out the general principles of what to
do, it's very unlikely that he would have had this spare brain
space to think about the detail of his situation on the night.

Individuals and organizations underestimate how much
mental capacity is used up by trying to deal with the unexpected from scratch. The simple rule should be, if your
business or organization is heavily reliant on a small number
of things for success, then you need to have plans in place
for how you would deal with things going wrong. If you
have one client who makes up most of your business, or one
supplier without whom the whole chain wouldn't work,
then you need to actively plan for life without them. If you
are approaching a pitch that has to go right, what would be
the worst three things that could happen? You'll never
utterly remove the potential for a curve ball, but you'll mini-

mize what you do get surprised by, and be better equipped for something truly unexpected. You need to keep in mind what you would do if you became the equivalent of a pilot without a plane. A useful exercise could be to get a team to list five unexpected things that could happen that are outside of your direct control and then how you might respond to them. The key here is not to focus on the potentially negative events, but in the power we have to change their outcomes by preparing appropriate responses to them.

How do we prepare our body and mind?

It's crucial that Dale had acknowledged that there was a chance, however slim, of being shot down, and had then prepared mentally. Furthermore, this meant that he'd also put thought into what his body, as well as his brain, would need if he ended up on the ground in enemy territory.

It was winter in Eastern Europe, which meant it was cold and wet, so not only did Dale wear extra socks but also lots of clothes – four layers. He knew that if any rescue attempt was delayed this would keep him warm, avoiding lowering his core body temperature towards hypothermia, which causes a drop in mental performance. He was flying in a warm jet, but he was dressed to survive on the cold, wet ground even when he was sitting in his snug cockpit. That's an image I want you to keep in mind. We all need to be mentally wearing an extra pair of socks, especially if we're sitting in our own version of a comfy cockpit.

Because of his SERE* training, Dale knew that his brain used a lot of energy and understood what nutrients it needed to function, so he had prepared physically too. He ensured his brain would have enough fuel by eating a big bowl of grape-nut cereal with extra dried cranberries before the flight; the complex carbohydrates that meal contained would release their energy slowly rather than the big but short spike you get from eating normal sugar. Brains run on glucose, and unless you can chain-eat sweets you want a form that feeds your system gradually, unlike the Polo Mints that sat on your exam desk for a quick mental boost. Dale also put extra energy reserves in his pockets, in the form of four chocolate, oatmeal and raisin power bars, in case his brain needed a top-up on the ground should he have to eject. Perhaps most importantly, he flew fully hydrated. This is key to brain function, as a reduction in hydration by only 1 per cent of your body weight can impair cognition. Being properly hydrated meant that Dale felt more alert and he knew that it would also reduce any potential shock symptoms. On top of being hydrated before take-off, he had twelve 4 oz (110 ml) water sachets packed for him in his survival kit, and he had also further prepared by adding

* In the UK, SERE stands for Survival (of the environment), Evasion (from enemy forces), Resistance (if captured) and Extraction (getting home via rescue or boot leather).

another litre and a half of his extra drinking water in small containers.

By doing all of this, even though the likelihood of needing it was vanishingly small, Dale had pre-planned for his brain's physiological needs. It's the sort of thing you could do too, like simply having a back-up snack bar deep in your laptop bag for the emergency scenario of missing lunch when you're on the way to an important meeting. People tend to think that the body and the mind are separate. I think it's mad that people go to a meeting or event that could change their lives feeling hungry or thirsty. We are chemical creatures and I don't care how well you've prepared a presentation or your answers to likely questions, if you've not given your brain the fuel it needs, you've not given yourself the best chance of success. We'll go into this in more detail in Chapter 3 as we look at our physiological limits, but it bears emphasizing at this point: if you're doing something important hungry or thirsty, you're fighting with one arm tied behind your back.

Try and give yourself a parachute moment

As Dale dangled in the night air below his parachute he quickly assessed his predicament. He knew that his shoot-down had been so quick that he'd been unable to use the aircraft radio to let anyone know. He knew that his jet was so stealthy that there wasn't a blip for anyone to see disappearing from their airborne control aircraft's radar screens. He knew he'd been flying on his own, so no wingman had witnessed what had happened to let others know. He knew that the key to getting rescued from hostile territory was letting rescue forces know you need their help as soon as possible. Nobody else in the air that night knew that he'd been shot down.

There's not a lot you can do under an opened round parachute while you're slowly drifting down waiting to land, so Dale found the most useful way to bide his time. He checked his pockets. Practising this as a touch drill nightly on the ground back at his base before each sortie meant he knew exactly which of his multitude of pockets and flaps to reach for in the dark. He put his hand on his evasion radio.

Then Dale did something he'd never been taught to do; still hanging under his parachute, he took his evasion radio out of its pocket and called for help. Using an evasion radio is only something he'd ever been taught to do *after* a parachute landing; but Dale also knew that the radio's range was limited, and it could reach much further the higher up he was. So, he reasoned, why not call for help early?

Preparing, drilling, using what ifs – none of that means you then have to stick rigidly to a script. You need to be able to respond to the situation in front of you. If you've prepared for your boss to grill you in a certain way and they don't, change your approach. If they ask a different difficult question at the presentation, your pre-thinking will help you to find ways of answering the question that they do ask more quickly. Importantly, Dale was only able to free up the brain space to improvise because he wasn't having to come up with entirely new responses to everything else prior to that. He already knew which pocket his radio was in. Our goal should be to give ourselves the best chance of having a parachute moment.

For Dale, this was absolutely essential. After all, he was about to be hunted by a highly motivated force (that he'd just bombed) for which he was the ultimate propaganda prize. Within a minute of exploding out of his crippled jet and while still dangling under his parachute in a cold, dark, enemy sky, Dale was talking to distant fellow pilots on his hand-held evasion radio. He knew the Serbs would be listening in, so it took a while for him to convince the friendlies about what was happening and explain where he was, without giving the whole game away. You can imagine their surprise; 'Stealth bombers don't get shot down, do they?' Finally, he was able to convince them he needed help and roughly where to find him. He put the radio back into its pocket. One less job on his to-do list. Still top of that list: don't get captured.

Getting your bearings

The best way to not get caught is to stay one step ahead of the people looking for you. So Dale got back to finding out as much as he could about his new environment, developing his situational awareness, or 'SA'. He orientated himself by cross-referencing features he could see on the ground through the cloud gaps against what he remembered from the map of the area on his squadron briefing-room wall. He orientated all that against the North Star, Polaris, which he found by using part of the Great Bear constellation – the asterism called the Plough – known to Americans as the Big Dipper.

If you ever fancy finding north this way, here's what Dale did, although I recommend practising it during a clear night on the ground before you try it dangling under a parachute over enemy territory. The seven stars in the Big Dipper are shaped like a ladle, with a ★ three-star handle on the left and a four-star, squareish bowl on the right (a bit like a less straight version of this · · · : :). By following the line of the two 'pointer' stars on the right-hand side of the square bowl upwards, you can find the Pole Star, true north. The distance between the upper pointer star and the Pole Star is roughly five times that between the two pointer stars (where the ★ is in the text above, bet you wondered why that was there at first). The Pole Star will be near the end of the imaginary line that you draw, brighter than the others near it. The Big Dipper moves around the Pole Star all night as the Earth turns, so it might be at a different angle in the sky when you look for it, but the technique stays the same.

When something unexpected happens, often we don't feel in any state to deal with further new information. That's when we need to do our equivalent of finding the North Star, so that we can orientate ourselves in our new environment. We need to go back to first principles and get the best information that we can, however we can, so we can start to understand our situation. Under pressure, there is often the temptation to limit information, to go into a bunker mentality, but that's exactly the time we need to be building up our store of knowledge. If the online finance system drops out, we need to go back to paper until it's up and running. If the email is on the fritz, we all need to be on the phones. Even though every part of your brain will be screaming that you need to take flight, don't let a bad situation be an excuse to put your head in the sand and freeze. You can't navigate a situation if you have no information, so work out what your North Star is, your anchor point, and rejoin the fight.

Once he had increased his knowledge of the general area, Dale looked out for specific threats. As he broke through the bottom layer of cloud at about 2,000 feet he could make out much more detail of the country he was about to enter, uninvited. He spotted a large road with four lanes and quite a bit of traffic. He also noted that there were several other roads, and assessed them all as barriers or obstacles to any mobile evasion he might have liked to attempt. He saw that the countryside in between was flat farmland with a few ditches and areas of low scrub, which would make finding somewhere good to hide difficult. The area was far from ideal in evasion terms. And then he noticed that he was drifting towards the major road – a parachute landing into rush-hour traffic would be hard to keep quiet – so he adjusted his harness and started to aggressively steer himself away from the road and its immediate threat of people and capture.

Changing mindset

As he neared the ground, Dale picked out a subtle dip, a piece of cover, that he would try to hide in after landing, choosing it as an out-of-direct-sight spot to get himself and his gear ready for the long night ahead. Dale was already changing his mental outlook.

Five minutes earlier he had been a pilot flying a warm, dry, clean state-of-the-art jet. Because of all the thorough mental preparation he'd done before this and every other previous flight he was able to rapidly switch mindset, not to one of a victim of circumstance passively letting events unfold around him, but to one driving those events and making his own informed choices. He'd mentally rehearsed his own actions in dire circumstances enough to increase his own adaptability to unlikely situations; he'd 'trained-in' that capacity. His world was about to change to one more familiar to a ground soldier than a fighter pilot, but he was ready for it and knew what to do. Most importantly, he'd been able to let his friends know, and they could start work early on getting him home. Any second now, his new office would be a cold, dark, wet and grimy ditch.

After he landed, Dale's parachute started to get dragged by the stiff breeze, so he released his shoulder straps one at a time, which let all the air out of the parachute and collapsed it, so that it was no longer pulling him along the ground. Then he rolled onto his stomach in the ploughed field and lay motionless, listening and *tuning-in* to his new world. He was less than fifty metres from the busy road he'd seen in his descent and he lay there silently for almost a minute, just watching and listening. No cars stopped.

So he gathered all his gear, hid his parachute under his upturned dark-green life raft in the bottom of a furrow,* and weighted them down with dirt to prevent the wind revealing them later. Then he moved off to his chosen spot, making sure to only tread in the base of the plough furrows and leave the soil crests undisturbed.

Dale knew how to minimize the amount of disturbance he was creating, and therefore how to minimize his chances of being found and captured, because he'd been trained to. All military aircrew get survival training, and this can

---

* The small survival packs under ejection seats even contain a life raft.

include how to survive in enemy territory. Unfortunately for Dale, it was over twenty years since he'd done his SERE training course – it's more frequent nowadays – but because he'd taken that training seriously, it provided him with, in his words: 'a tremendous foundation of skills, considerations and equipment familiarity. It gives an experience of how to think and what to do.' How to think, and importantly how to *rethink*.

As Dale said in an interview afterwards:

> Right after ejection I switched my whole mindset and attitude from cosy pilot in a cockpit, to now I've got to be a high-speed covert special ops, special tactics, you know, low-signature kind of guy on the ground. And again, I changed my whole attitude towards that; that is how I have to be, absolutely minimizing movement, sound, anything that could compromise my position. So unless I was active with something, which included using the latrine, I decided, 'You know what? I should be hugging the eastern slope of this shallow irrigation ditch facing, roughly, north, motionless, kind of spread out.' Try not to look like a man-shape, head below line of sight of the horizon. Fortunately, that is the position I was in.[7]

As we'll see when we deal with more extended periods of survival later in the book, being adaptable and able to switch your mindset is essential.

When the unexpected strikes, we can waste time and energy feeling hard done by. We can get annoyed by the fact that all those scientists hadn't done their job right in creating the perfect stealth fighter. We can curse our luck in getting shot down. We can allow ourselves to be crushed by the overwhelming odds against evading the soldiers tracking us. Or we can take ownership of the situation in front of us. It's not our fault, but it is our reality. We all like to think that we're not the sort of person that bad things happen to and that if they do, they're certainly not down to us, but we can't allow that to tip over into not taking responsibility for our own lives. Events are not down to us, but dealing with them is.

If you're used to running the second biggest company in your sector and now you're eighth, deal with it. You're eighth biggest now, what are your new goals? If you're used to sailing through appraisals at the top of the class, but this time you've taken away a shopping list of things to work on, that's where you are now.

You can either keep thinking of yourself as a pilot without a plane, or you can change your mindset and start walking in the furrows. The quickest route to losing motivation in any situation and therefore to failure is to bring an old mindset with you; having impossible goals removes any sense of success or progression from that point onwards.

Preparing to remember

Dale prepared a document before his flight outlining what he planned to do if he had to evade capture by enemy forces, all written in the first person; lots of 'I will . . .' to make it stick in his memory when he read it. He'd refreshed and reviewed it in his mind's eye before every mission, so he was continuously mentally rehearsing the actions for his own worst-case night out. I'm sure that it's exactly this tactic of regular mental preparation which kept the physical training from twenty years earlier fresh in his memory files for when he needed it.

It used to be the done thing for a business to carry out a Strengths, Weaknesses, Opportunities and Threats (SWOT) analysis. But it's my experience, in most cases, that this often becomes little more than a box-ticking exercise. (Strengths: we're good at this sort of thing; Weaknesses: sometimes we're not the best; Opportunities: if it works, it'll make us lots of money; Threats: it might not work.) I think it's often the abstraction that's unhelpful here. I would replace SWOT analysis with a much more personalized set of 'if X happens, I will do Y' scenarios. We need to make our response to unexpected events active, not passive, and personal, so we take ownership of our new reality, like Dale was able to; creating an 'I will' to each of our 'what ifs'.

Dale was to spend almost eight hours evading a growing force of hunters that night, ranging from front-line troops with helicopters, to the arguably more dangerous local villagers and their dogs. He was eventually rescued from his ordeal thanks to the combined bravery and skill of a large team of specialists, who risked their own lives to penetrate hostile airspace and pluck him from the enemy's backyard. But there wouldn't have been any rescue if it hadn't been for Dale knowing what to do before, approaching and during the situation. He adapted to his environment smoothly through great preparation and planning, both mental and physical.

Mental rehearsals

So, we've seen how the correct building of 'muscle memory' helps to hardwire life-saving reactions into our brains for any real-time, worst-case scenario. Mental rehearsals are invaluable and, if you get the chance, physical rehearsals can be priceless. Firstly, because we remember things more easily when we learn them in context, when lots of our senses are firing to encode a many-faceted experience. This has been proven by researchers, who tested the theory by comparing learning on land and learning underwater in scuba gear. They found that subjects performed better when they were tested in the same context in which they learned the information, i.e. underwater learners tested better underwater.[8] This study didn't prove that we learn better on land or underwater; it proved that we access memories better if we create them in the context that we are then tested in later. Which is why, although it's important to have those away days for teambuilding, it's equally important to have training in your organization that actually mirrors *what you do* and *where you do it*. If you're not gathering your teams together and placing real-world scenarios in front of them to solve as part of their training, you're not helping them lay down behaviours and responses in the best possible way. If you're not cross-examining, asking what-ifs, demanding alternative scenarios, you're leaving yourself open to the unexpected always happening.

Train yourself to see unanimous support for a course of action as a warning sign, not a positive. After all, as we'll see, very often when we're confronted with unfamiliar or difficult decisions and that feeling of threat kicks in, our brains take the wrong shortcuts. If you're in a room full of people all agreeing the same thing, then there's every chance that groupthink will lead to a less-than-optimal choice. If I set a new challenge out in the wilderness, something that we haven't pre-drilled, and start hearing people say, 'obviously this is how we should do it', or 'there's only one way to do this', I remind them that not only is the first choice not necessarily always the best one – because our brains are taking the wrong sort of shortcuts to similar but not necessarily appropriate options – but that if we only ever did what we'd done before, we'd never learn anything new. We'll never be able to do away with groupthink entirely, but we can always try to challenge it.

Improving preparation

A good exercise for getting into a preparation mindset is one that commercial airline pilots practise when checking in to a new hotel. Long-haul commercial pilots wake up on different continents on a weekly basis, so they are almost continuously in strange environments. While they know through regular practise how to evacuate an airliner, they don't always know the best evacuation routes for the hotel that they are staying in between return flights. Their exercise uses the same fundamental concepts we saw above, and can be applied by us when we arrive somewhere unfamiliar too. Once you've settled into your hotel room, check the little map by the door for where the emergency stairs and exits are, in case you smell smoke in the night or are abruptly awoken by the hotel fire alarm. That is step one. Step two: walk the route to the exit – to cement it in your mind as a kind of touch-drill before you need to do it in anger. Focus on where to turn at corridor junctions and how far away the doors are.

This could literally save your life, but it's also a great way to practise getting into a mindset of equipping yourself with the information you need to deal with scenarios that you face. When I work with mixed groups of civilians and military, you can tell who's military straight away. Anyone who's been in the services wants to equip themselves with as much information about what we're going to do as possible. We're going into which forest? How big is it? How far away? What do we know about what's in it? What will we be carrying? Most civilians would be halfway over the fence by the time you'd finished saying 'forest'. This is because a key part of any military plan is trying to minimize the 'risk to life' in the event of things heading south. Preparation isn't an optional extra, it's the most important foundation of everything that follows. By narrowing the window of the unknown, you increase your chances of success. This is a habit that can be developed, practised and improved. The greater the number of appropriate reactions we can drill into ourselves, the quicker we'll respond and the more spare mental capacity – in the form of freed-up 'working memory' – we'll have to tackle the unexpected details and contingencies that we couldn't have predicted.

We need to try and drill as much as we can, so we free our slow brains up to work on the things we genuinely can't prepare for.

With that in mind, I am often amazed by the amount of people who can't use the basic tools they need to do their jobs. I imagine many of you who work in busy offices have heard numerous questions like 'how do you send an attachment?', 'how do you make spreadsheets do X?'. Think of the mental bandwidth being taken up by not knowing how to perform relatively simple, day-to-day tasks. Asking definitively how to do something simple might feel demeaning, but once you know it, you know it. Then drill it. You never hear an astronaut say, 'Oh yeah, I always wondered what that warning light meant.'

In the survival world, we try and have a culture where there really is no such thing as a stupid question. If you're in any doubt how or why to do something, ask. And then make sure you can remember the answer next time. When you're in the sort of extreme environments we're operating in, it can be the difference between success and failure.

An easy exercise when you've finished this chapter would be to go away and find out one thing you're slightly ashamed you don't already know how to do at work. By asking for some tips or advice from someone who does the task every day you'll normally get a positive response; you're showing interest in something that is important to them, and most people really are happy to help. If in doubt, ask; it'll be far less embarrassing in the long run.

Rehearse

The more frequently you access those brain files through rehearsing their contents, the easier they'll be to retrieve when you really need them. An easy one we can all apply is letting colleagues know if a deadline isn't going to be achievable. We'll come back to this, but most people try to 'fix' situations in work on their own, and often the result is letting people know about problems far too late for them to do anything about it. We get bogged down in why something is late, feelings of guilt, responsibility or avoidance. A ticking clock, with threats of negative outcomes, will immediately make our threat system engage and we'll feel tempted to flee. If you're not going to be able to make the deadline, don't panic and avoid thinking about the task or blame whatever has happened to put you behind. You need to be able to change your mindset. You're not going to make that deadline, so adapt, work out one you can hit and then tell everyone who needs to know. Your job isn't to absorb the information passively, it's to pass it on actively. For every project, you can mentally practise what you'll do if a deadline slips before it happens, so precious brain energy isn't being wasted if and when it does occur. Dale was only rescued from his predicament because he let the right people know early.

Homework

Here's another way of road-testing how effective a small amount of preparation can be. The next time you land in a strange country it's unlikely to be at night by parachute, but you can employ the same principles that Dale did to make your arrival at an unfamiliar airport as smooth as possible. As your plane begins its descent and the cabin lights come on, you can start to orientate yourself in your new environment. Some airlines have maps of their terminals in the in-flight magazine; take a picture of it with your mind's-eye or your smartphone. These can be really helpful for making tight connections or even finding out where to go for the hotel shuttle buses.

After landing, you'll need to have the important stuff to hand, a kind of arrival touch-drill. Don't be the person covered in travel pillows and headphones, pockets bulging. They are the ones that the airport underworld will target, their air of chaos attracting touts. Put your wallet in a separate, preferably zipped pocket, and have your passport in a pocket on its own. If you need cash, have a few smaller denomination bills in a pocket too; you don't want to have to show the world all your trip funds in one go at the vehicle stands later. Try to remove any expensive-looking watches or jewellery; the only people who will be admiring those once you've landed are the wrong types. It's also a really good idea to have the address of where you're staying printed out on a piece of paper – minus all your personal info – to show to any official taxi or shuttle bus service rep. That avoids pronunciation misunderstandings or even being taken to somewhere that sounds like the right place, but leaves you on the wrong side of town. Now you're ready to land.

Once you've actually entered the new country through passport control, and before you get to the busy arrivals hall, check to see if your phone works, then put it back into a deep pocket in case you need it later. If you know you won't need to use it, put it into airplane mode to save on any roaming charges until you forage out some Wi-Fi.*

As you enter the throng at arrivals, don't be the person who looks lost. Remember the route from your airport map to the shuttle area; knowing where that is and striding for it confidently lowers your chances of being singled out by the many touts who victim-spot at transport hubs. They know that the majority of fresh arrivals will be a little over-whelmed and unfamiliar with the layout straight after col-lecting their luggage and may be more susceptible to direction, even if that is simply someone saying 'taxi, taxi, taxi' on loop and hustling them towards a vehicle. Looking confident by knowing where you're headed, and therefore 'more at home', allows you to blend in.

There is one further benefit to walking tall and confi-dently. Research has shown that when we occupy a little more physical space with our bodies, spreading ourselves out rather than hunching up, subtle changes to our brain

---

* As important to teenagers as air is to humans, Wi-Fi hotspots can normally be spotted from afar by the number of yoofs screengazing.

chemistry occur. Adopting confident body language, what social psychologist Amy Cuddy has dubbed 'power poses', not only makes us feel better, it makes us *perform* better.[9] Cuddy's research has shown that adopting 'power poses' for as little as two minutes can also lower our cortisol levels, and we know too much cortisol impedes our mental agility.

Your onward travel from the airport is best planned ahead of your trip, but if you didn't have time then there's a chance that hotel shuttle buses could be coordinated from a help desk within the airport. If you need to exchange any money at this point, only use recognizable exchange bureau brands, not the many dodgy characters hanging out just short of those storefronts.

Language barriers may be the next issue, and if you don't know any key phrases in the local lingo then a 'pointee-talkee' can be very helpful. They are printed cards with many different icons that will allow you to speak in that universal language; pictures. But be careful how you point to things like images of buses; in some countries of the world an extended index finger is very offensive, so use a cheap pen. If you can't find a transport service desk, ask an airline rep about shuttle buses. This is where your printed-out hotel address is most useful.

If that doesn't work, it's time to leave the airport and get a normal taxi. Only go for the official taxi rank, with proper marked cabs lined up ready to go. In some parts of the world there will be hustlers trying to get you into their colleague's plain, unlicensed vehicles; be polite but don't let them handle you, or your luggage.

Finally, walk confidently to the taxi stand, even if you don't feel that way inside. Yet. A tiny amount of preparation for any difficulties you might face will free up enormous amounts of mental capacity for dealing with everything else. Try adding some of these shortcuts into your airport routine and see what happens. Rather than arriving at your hotel in full threat mode, making poor decisions, you'll have freed up the mental space to begin your trip properly.

Summary

→ Prepare your brain. It uses 20 per cent of your energy so it needs fuel. Stock up on complex carbs before you do anything that demands a lot of thought. Your brain needs water to work; a reduction in hydration by only 1 per cent of your body weight can impair cognition, so stay hydrated when you're making crucial decisions.

→ Prepare for worst-case scenarios and free up brain power. Most people roll their eyes at SWOT analysis and treat it as a box-ticking exercise. You need a working culture where people are open and proactive about the risks they might face and what individuals will do to minimize them.

→ Assess the threats in your surroundings by going through some 'what if . . .' scenarios, then draft some 'I will . . .' responses and mentally rehearse them. If you don't it'll take your brain 8–10 seconds to generate a novel riposte on the spot.

→ If you're feeling stressed, try breathing exercises or chewing to calm down. Chewing before or during a high-pressure event will also lower your cortisol levels.

→ Mentally and physically rehearse any vital actions with touch-drills to make them stick, even dry run the walk or journey to an important meeting so that you can work through any contingency routes and avoid being late on the day.

→ We access memories better if we created them in the context that we are then tested in later; so practise using a paper map and compass to find your position while you're actually out hiking. The batteries in your satnav may die, leaving the map and compass as your only option.

→ It's impossible to know everything, no matter how experienced you are. If you're with another person, don't be afraid to defer to their expertise. Learning to rely on each other is vital to surviving with someone else.

→ Follow the tips above to ensure you land safely in strange new places. Once you begin to apply a clear-sighted look at risk in your life, you'll see how many 'unexpected' events are actually predictable and can be prepared for. You'll free up mental capacity for the important stuff.

We've seen how important pre-planning is in controlling the variables in unforeseen circumstances. But how do we best decide what to do and in what order? For that we need to go back to basics and work out what's going to harm us first.

Chapter 2

PRIORITIZATION

The pilot's eyes darted inside again to look at the gauges; the fuel in their small plane was running out. Off to the north-east the tropical sun shone brightly, and the many fluffy cumulous clouds that had bubbled up cast dark patches of shadow onto the sea. The pilot looked down and decided to land. This wasn't the airfield on the flight plan, but the small flat reef at the tip of the deserted tropical island's lagoon would have to do; ditching in the wide expanses of the shark-infested Pacific would be far worse. They had strained their eyes onto the shimmering sea for too long now, their airfield was nowhere to be seen, so landing on this reef was their best chance of survival. The pilot prepared the aircraft; she eased back on its throttles and lowered the flaps to begin their descent.

When Amelia Earhart disappeared during her attempt to be the first woman to fly around the world in 1937, she was an international A-list superstar, a household name. She was a pioneer of aviation and equality, and as she flew from west to east around our planet in her twin-engined Electra plane, she had all of the latest 1930s technology fitted inside it. She was at the forefront of developments in radio navigation, where aircraft are guided to small points on a map by invisible radio beams. Along with her navigator, Fred Noonan, Amelia was attempting one of the more hazardous legs of the trip when she had taken off on the second of July. They had already completed two-thirds of their global circumnavigation; now they were crossing vast stretches of open water by island-hopping, heading back to the United States.

This flight from New Guinea was to take them to a landing strip on Howland Island in the wide blue Pacific, roughly halfway to Hawaii. A two-mile long, low-lying green speck of an island, on a vast ocean covered with island-sized patches of darker cloud shadows.

At her destination, the US Navy had been sending out invisible radio handrails to funnel the small aircraft towards its tiny target, and were listening for any transmissions that Amelia made as she tried to find them. As you read this today, hundreds of passenger airliners are crossing the Pacific in all directions and finding city airports with ease – modern airports are not dissimilar in size to the whole of Howland Island – in the dark, in fog, in torrential rain. In 1937, Amelia was a pioneer, but the technology wasn't perfect. Howland could hear her calling as she approached, but she couldn't quite tune in to their direction beams. Her voice came through ever more crisp and clear on the US Navy speakers, she was getting tantalizingly close. Then, at around 7.40 a.m., they heard: 'We must be on you but cannot see you . . . but gas is running low.'

As the eyes of Amelia and her navigator strained to spot the island, and the Navy tried in vain to reach them, her fuel ran lower. The radio navigation equipment wasn't working, the Navy sent beams out but she couldn't receive them. She turned and began to fly on a more north-to-south line in the hopes of sighting Howland. And then she disappeared.

Imagine the most internationally famous female celebrity you know of vanishing today. In July 1937, that was Amelia, and the story shook the world. The US Government launched a Navy search costing millions of dollars; no one was found. It remains a mystery to this day, with the inevitable collection of online conspiracy theories thrown in as possible answers.

But there's enough evidence from one of the many theories to convince me of where Amelia ended her global flight. Radio calls were heard after the time when her aircraft's fuel should have been long exhausted. Because of its construction, her aircraft's radio antennas would not have worked if it was afloat at sea; she had to be transmitting for rescue from land. When several of these transmissions were received in different parts of the Pacific, the lines showing the directions they came from were plotted onto a chart. The radio lines crossed in a scattered patch of islands called the Phoenix group, about 350 nautical miles (over 600 km) to the south-east of her intended destination. One of those islands – Gardner Island, now called Nikumaroro – is on the track that Amelia was flying to search for her destination. It has a flat reef, flat enough to land an aircraft on. If she had landed on the reef she could have used her plane's radio to make the calls for help that were heard in the days after her disappearance. These calls for help continued for several days – at the same times as low tide on Nikumaroro – until increasingly higher tides lifted the aircraft and floated it off the reef to sink in deeper waters offshore. In my opinion, these calls for help had to have come from Amelia.

Because of the triangulated radio calls, the Navy dispatched the battleship USS *Colorado* to search the Phoenix Islands. Once it eventually arrived on scene, a week after she disappeared, its aircraft swooped low to look for signs of Amelia's plane. At Nikumaroro, a pilot from the *Colorado* reported: 'signs of recent habitation were clearly visible but repeated circling and zooming failed to elicit any answering wave from possible inhabitants and it was finally taken for granted that none were there.' He was not to know that Nikumaroro had been uninhabited since 1892, when it had been planted with coconut palms.

Your desert island

I want you to imagine you are in Amelia Earhart's situation. Marooned on an island. What would you do first? Look for shelter, look for water, look for food, try to make a fire? Take a minute now to note down your order. One of our first tasks when we're out of the immediate impact of a survival event is to come up with what we do next. But often, the brain needs a little help. This is because . . .

Your brain is bad at prioritizing

The reason for this ties back to something we've already touched on – that to save time, our brains often boil things down to threat and reward. We seek to avoid threats and we seek to do things that bring us the most immediate reward. It's the reason why so many commuters can't stop playing games on their mobile phone, rather than finally finishing their book, however much they're enjoying it. If you leave it up to your brain, it will choose that little hit of dopamine it gets solving those quick problems, over the more satisfying slow burn of the unfolding knowledge or the novelty of the story in your book. This makes sense when you think about the evolutionary benefits of responding to the immediate threat or reward for our ancestors. But it's a real problem now, especially since time and time again, studies have shown that the further in the future we perceive the benefits of a decision to be, the worse we are at making that decision.[10] We have to learn to balance this out by making the long-term benefits feel more important. So let's look at what we actually need and the order we need it in.

Your bodily needs

Let's take the example of you, at rest, on a normal day indoors. Energy-wise your body's on tick-over, your environment is controlled and comfortable, and you have access to the stuff you're used to consuming. During this day you'll breathe on average twelve to twenty lungfuls every minute – which adds up to 11,000 litres of air – the volume of a cement truck. You are warm-blooded and you need to maintain your body's core temperature of 37°C to stay alive. At rest, in a benign climate, this uses the energy in your body at a rate of around 100W, the output of a small lightbulb, and over a day that can burn around 1,500 calories.* Just performing at these base metabolic rates you'll

---

* Basal metabolic rates vary from person to person. If you want to work out yours, here are the sums you need. For women: BMR = 10 x weight (kg) + 6.25 x height (cm) – 5 x age (years). Then subtract 161. For men, the same sum but instead of subtracting 161 at the end, add five. The answer is the calories you need for a day of total inactivity, which normally come in the form of Pringles.

use up 1.5 litres of water in a day, 500 ml each through respiration, perspiration and urination – breathing, sweating and peeing.

So, what if you lost access to these resources? Without air, or specifically the oxygen in it, you'll survive for about three minutes, unless you're a highly trained free-diver. You contain about 5 litres of warm blood, and if you develop a leak then a loss of 40 per cent of your total blood volume, roughly 2 litres, is generally fatal without medical intervention. And it's *warm* blood: not too hot, not too cold, Goldilocks. If your core temperature goes just 2.3°C above or below 37°C your performance starts to degrade; you stop controlling your situation. Get too cold or too hot, by as little as a 5°C change in core temperature, and you could be unconscious in minutes, dead in hours.

But what if you still had air and were uninjured and at the right temperature, how long have you got then? Even if you do nothing, just running your body's engine on baseline tick-over demands oil and fuel in the form of water and nutrients. For your body to run efficiently you need to have the right level of hydration; the right amount of water in it. Depending on your build and size this will vary, but as a proportion we are made up of roughly two thirds water. If we don't keep topping that up as we lose our 1.5 litres a day on tick-over, after a few days your engine will eventually seize up. What about fuel? We know that our bodies are two thirds water, which for an 80 kg person equates to over

50 litres. We also know that our body's core needs to be kept at 37°C. Food energy is measured in calories; in simple terms, a calorie is the amount of energy that is required to raise the temperature of one litre of water by one degree Celsius. Working in normal outdoor temperatures this means it can require 2,000–2,500 calories of fuel a day. If you're working in typical Arctic temperatures of around -20°C, the bigger difference between outside and what your core needs means that your requirements can easily go up to 6,000–8,000 calories a day. Dr Mike Stroud, when he walked across Antarctica with Ranulph Fiennes, calculated their daily burn to be as high as a whopping 11,000 calories (or seventeen Burger King Whoppers).

We ideally need a balanced diet, but in terms of what fuel to put in your tank the different components of food have different energy values. Carbohydrates and proteins contain roughly 4 calories per gram, whereas fats have around 9 calories per gram; they are much more energy rich. Because fats are a high-octane fuel, we're also now hardwired to like the taste of fatty foods on our palates – it's your body's way of telling you that this is a good energy source, eat more of it.

What if you run out of fuel? Well, if you stop eating you will start to use your body's easy-access energy stored in the blood, liver and muscles, and then you'll switch to deeper reserves. This will firstly be your body's fat; when that's gone, your muscles, until there's nothing left – normally a matter of weeks (forty to sixty days) if you're sedentary. It's a bit like Phileas Fogg; burning the decking and fittings of his ship for fuel to get back from his trip around the world inside eighty days.

To summarize and generalize: if you can't breathe or are bleeding heavily, time to death is in **minutes**, uninjured at extremes of temperature it's in **hours**, without any drinking water death takes **days**, and without food, **weeks**.

I've performed this thought experiment on a variety of people, and I can tell you that the vast majority without survival training get at least two things in completely the wrong order. Leaving aside the assumption that we can breathe and we're not leaking blood, almost everyone then puts food too high up the list and shelter/temperature management too low. When I tell people you can survive without eating food for weeks, but you die within hours at extremes of temperature, they can't quite believe it. I believe the reason for this ties into the way our brain deals with rewards. Getting food and eating it is a much more immediate, tangible reward than the longer-term benefits of making a shelter now to use later. Anyone who's ever left putting their tent up at a music festival until it gets dark so they can enjoy some beers in the sun knows what I'm talking about.

Now, let's imagine how your decisions might play out in real life if we listen to our untrained brain.

You're hot, hungry and thirsty, you have some water left over in your crashed plane but no food, so you decide to try and catch some fish first. You sit out in the sun for a couple of hours, sweating, without catching anything. You realize that you're out of water, so start to explore the beach, to try and find some fresh water running into the sea, but can't find any and the sun starts to go down. As your sweat starts to cool, you shiver and realize you need to collect some firewood. By the time you've done that, you stumble around in the dark, trying to find the best place to shelter, eventually finding somewhere you think is suitable. You're shivering, thirsty, in a cloud of mosquitoes, trying and failing to light a fire and as you do, you hear the drone of an aircraft overhead as you sit invisible in the darkness.

In survival, we have an acronym for our priorities – PLAN – for just this reason. Here's how it works.

Get a PLAN

Protection

If you haven't been injured, your first concern is keeping your temperature regulated. The first layer of protection from extremes of temperature – preserving that vital 37°C – and from other hazards, is your clothing. It's protecting you from rain, wind, shine, scratches and stings. If the conditions are bad then you need to improve your chances by controlling your immediate environment beyond what you're wearing too. This can be as simple as moving out of the wind to the leeward side of some cover, or finding trees to shelter from the worst of the midday heat, or as complicated as weaving a hammock from vines to sleep away from the biting insects of the jungle floor. Find the most efficient point on that spectrum, and you're obtaining shelter. Once shelter has been addressed, if the resulting palace could still be improved, then lighting a small fire will boost your morale, add warmth and protect you from things that bite, be they mosquito or wolf-sized. All of these defensive screens to your body – first aid, clothing, shelter and fire – are grouped together in that order under the title **Protection** in our list of survival priorities.*

Location, location, location

Next on the list of survival priorities is **Location**; in this context, the art of being found. As we know, we can survive for days without water and weeks without food, so there's no real need to elevate their priority in your plan of action. It is important, however, to remember that if you don't get back from being stranded you're not actually a survivor. You need to get to safety – either by being rescued or by making your own way out. This is something that tends to get missed out on survival shows, where catching unusual animals to eat

---

* In very cold weather, light a fire before starting on a shelter. That way you can warm your hands if they get cold – much easier than trying to light a fire with already chilled fingers.

can have more visual impact than putting energy into letting others know that you need assistance. But prioritizing rescue above water and food makes so much sense because once you've put your effort into successfully getting found by rescuers, you can ask them to bring beer and pizza anyway. Whereas if you missed the signalling-for-help part out in your plan you'll stay marooned forever, living off monkey anuses, or whatever else is on your TV survival menu. So, getting found – 'located' by rescuers – is next in your order of business. Putting your finite energy into this task above finding water and food makes for a speedy return to civilization. That's why Location is second after Protection in the priority list. It's incredibly important to put enough effort into getting rescued, or finding your own way out; you don't want to set up a permanent camp, you haven't just found your 'for ever' home. However comfortable you think you might be at first, any strategy of not trying for rescue will ultimately be unsustainable.

Acquiring water and food

Once you've come up with a way of attracting and holding the attention of would-be rescuers, and devised a means of directing them to you, you can start to think about **Acquiring sustenance**. You'll need at least 1.5 litres of drinking water a day just to keep up your baseline functions, and any exertion or extremes of climate can increase this figure dramatically. Water needs to be found, collected, any impurities dealt with, and then safely stored, and it takes a lot more effort and time than you'd think. Once Protection, Location and water have been sorted, it's finally time to think about what's for dinner. You may have some food with you, or you may have to find it all. In order to keep things simple, try to collect the easiest stuff first before embarking on any Rambo-esque hunting missions, knife between teeth. The things your body needs from food fall into one of five categories: fat, protein, carbohydrates, vitamins and minerals, and the good stuff is often hidden in plain sight.

Navigation

The last thing on your checklist of priorities is **Navigation**. It's usually always best to stay near where you first became isolated, especially if that's a broken-down vehicle, as that's easier to spot than a person. The exception to this rule of thumb is when staying put increases the risk of harm to you, like if your crash site or similar is exposed to bad weather conditions or dangerous environmental factors, such as flooding or falling debris. In situations like that, you'd refer to the P of PLAN: Protection. Once you're in a safe area, your energy needs to be focused on further addressing the priorities of survival – Protection, Location, Acquiring water and food – outlined above. It would be very unusual for all of that to be within arm's reach, so you'll need to be able to orientate yourself to your surroundings and use very simple navigation techniques to get back to your focal point – your home base.

Now you have a PLAN

So there you have the survival priorities of **P**rotection, **L**ocation, **A**cquiring water and food and **N**avigation. Having a checklist of priorities like this makes it easier for us to think rationally and formulate a clear plan of action, wherever we are. What we spend our energy on first should be the most important thing, the top of the list, preventing us wasting our limited time and resources. This helps us combat the fact that our brains, in general, are much better at making short-term decisions than long-term ones. What PLAN does is force us to upend that and confront the actual benefits of each course of action, and prioritize accordingly.

The bones of your PLAN, wherever you are, should be based on the simple question 'what will harm me first?' I can sense you thinking, *That's all very well, but how often am I going to be stranded on a desert island?* So let's look at a scenario that's probably more familiar.

Castaway in the woods

You've been out forest hiking all day alone, you feel footsore but happy, and as you approach the final ridge of the new trail you're following, you look forward to seeing the trailhead parking lot as the sun sets across the valley below. Clearing the final trees onto the ridge, the sun isn't ahead as you'd expected but way off to the left. Worse, the parking lot isn't ahead of you at all, but a steep and deep gorge is there instead; it's bottom is already in dark shadow, hidden from the dipping sun. These are the moments where the decisions we make about what to do next are vital.

Let's assume that our hiker isn't loaded down with lots of gear to camp out, and equally likely – as it was planned to be a day hike – they haven't got a flashlight in their jacket pocket. Often in the media we hear about folk in exactly this kind of scenario, who react uncalmly to instinctive urges to keep pushing on into the night, and, if they're lucky, emerge days or weeks later, or the unlucky ones who don't make it out.

What I've heard from those I train, and what I read about again and again when looking into real world survival stories, is that so many people react to these moments by doing the equivalent of wandering up and down the beach, moving back and forth between gathering sticks and foraging for food, vaguely looking for water, never building their shelter. They are, in effect, passively letting their brains decide what order to do things in. And as we probably realize by now, that is not the best idea.

What we need to do is employ PLAN. Every situation and environment are subtly different, but we can boil things down to their essentials. Work out what is most important to get done first. (Hint: it's almost always not going to be the thing that feels immediately easiest, like charging back down the trail. Things our brains think of as easy are likely to be quick and, for most of us, it's very rarely the quick things that are most important.)

Create your own PLAN

Let's suppose you have somehow found yourself lost deep in a strange, darkening forest, miles from help. There's no point trying to get yourself unlost in the dark by walking further; it would only make the situation worse and possibly get you injured too. By avoiding the instinctive feeling to do that, you are beginning to Protect yourself, the P of PLAN. Instead, start positive action by using the remaining daylight to your advantage to create the most comfortable home for the night that you can – maintaining your body temperature will be critical.

If for some reason you don't think you'll be able to re-orientate yourself or retrace your route out in the morning – maybe you have injured your leg – then you also need to address Location, the L of PLAN, by trying to help rescuers find you.

In a less demanding kind of overnight scenario that's not complicated by injury, you're probably going to need to acquire more water in the morning, but you won't die if you don't eat, so we can be flexible enough to think about how we might Navigate our way out in daylight instead for now. So this is where you can focus on the relevant elements of your PLAN, list them out – preferably on paper – and give them more attention.

Get specific

Make the list items specific. PLAN could be further simplified to GR – Get Rescued – but that's not really going to help us prioritize or execute. Instead, we should follow the rule we saw when we were looking at pre-planning, and make things personal, specific, active and related to scenarios with 'What if . . .' questions and 'I will . . .' answers.

In fact, you can be even more specific than PLAN, because this is tailored to your exact scenario by you. You should be noting the number of pieces of firewood you're going to gather, and how much drinking water you need to acquire.

Tidy camp, tidy mind

As any survival instructor will tell you, keep your camp tidy! The quickest way to get your brain in a muddle is to mix up where things are. If you're ever feeling overwhelmed, sort out that living space. You don't need to go full Zen master, but make sure that there are separate areas for things, and that they feel ordered and deliberate.

Focus

Every time you think about letting something new creep in front of something on your task list, keep thinking of that idea of wandering back and forth on the beach, never accomplishing any one task, dropping the firewood as you realize you need water, being distracted by food as you look guiltily back towards your unfinished shelter. You don't want to finish every day shivering, being bitten by mosquitoes. In my experience of teaching survival, multi-tasking is a myth. Beyond two or three things, our brains start dropping something off to make room. It's much better to 'chunk' together similar tasks into small groups if you need to handle more than one problem at a time. Hunter-gatherers did one thing at a time – follow their advice. If you have to, collect similar types of tasks together, but where possible plan to single-task as much as you are possibly able to. I hear tell of people able to keep fifteen plates spinning all at once, but I don't think I've ever met one.

Using positive and negative framing

Generally, we need to make sure we're framing what we're doing as something positive that will lead to a goal in some way, not just escaping the negative. Fear of failure might work to some extent but it's nowhere near as good a long-term strategy as finding the rewards within what you do. And those rewards should be personal to you, rather than too abstract. Try and concentrate on the good things that will happen when you clear your big task, like making a bough bed, how good it will feel. You need to get that moment clear in your mind's eye in order to outweigh the effort it is going to take getting there.

Having said that, if I'm really avoiding doing something, like making a time-consuming hammock to keep me off the floor and away from anything living there, it can be useful to remember what the downside of not doing it would be – for instance, the night a colleague spent twisting tics out of his friend's unmentionables does wonders for my priorities.

What happened to Amelia?

Later in 1937, when a British group were exploring Niku-maroro, they found signs of a camp. Then in 1940, another British official found bones near an old campfire that were then measured and assessed by a doctor as belonging to a person of European ancestry. They also found a wooden box for a navigator's sextant. When these sites have been investigated from the 1990s onwards by researchers from TIGHAR, The International Group for Historic Aircraft

Recovery, they've found other fascinating items. Parts of a pair of shoes, similar to those worn by Amelia in photographs taken during her trip, were found in the shade under a tree near some old campfire charcoal.

Most interestingly, several small jars and bottles dating to the 1930s that were originally containers for women's cosmetics, plus parts of a make-up compact, have all been found at the site. One of the jars was broken, and a part from it found near turtle bones some distance away. Was Amelia improvising a cutting tool? Having spent some time myself on hot, arid, tropical coasts, the discovery of lotion bottles at the island camp that had been heated by fire at their base is a sure sign to me that they were used to try and distil seawater into drinking water.

Nikumaroro had no fresh water source in 1937, daytime temperatures can top 40°C, so there was only the seawater or rainwater available to drink, and several sea shells were laid out at the camp as if to catch rain. Near to that area in the 1940s, a US serviceman described finding an improvised construction – a tough canvas sheet lashed up on poles feeding into a metal collection tank. His drawing of it looked exactly like the many rain-catchers I've seen coastal survival students build over the last fifteen years.

Based on her radio transmissions, the US Navy aircraft's search timeline, and the artefacts found on Nikumaroro, Amelia managed to survive for days. But without rescue or a means of delivering herself from the island, ultimately, the best she could do was to sit in the hot shade on the waterless shore, where she eventually died of dehydration.

Amelia's remains have never been definitively identified, and recently soil samples have been taken from the island in the slim hope of finding DNA evidence. But for me the many other artefacts provide the clearest proof that at some point in the late 1930s a Western woman survived on a remote, uninhabited, waterless desert island for as long as she could. I use her story to remind myself that we can never plan for everything, but that until we find ourselves checkmated like Amelia, we should realize how much we can control. Who knows how the story would have ended if she'd used some of her initial energy to write a big 'HELP' on the beach?

I often get asked what the best practical survival training course to do is. My answer is always the same, and it ties in with the priorities we've just looked at. If anyone you're with ever has an injury causing loss of blood, or any other kind of body damage, having some good hands-on first-aid training will help you to help yourself and others. It's impossible to save a badly injured friend who's losing blood if you don't already know and have practised a few simple pressure application techniques; reading guidebooks on the spot won't help you fast enough, and the pages will stick together. The best example I know of first-aid training good karma is Dr Heimlich. You probably recognize his name as the man who, back in 1974, invented a manoeuvre to stop people from choking. In 2016, the doctor, then aged ninety-six, used the technique he invented and saved the life of a choking woman. It's far better to know first aid and not need it for years, than need it now, but not know how.

Summary

→ Know your vulnerabilities and have them jotted out mentally in order of importance – you can then scan for any immediate threats to you much more effectively. Even better, you can work on ways to bolster any vulnerable areas and even turn them into strengths.

→ Use the survival question 'What will harm me first?' in your everyday life by asking 'What's the single most important thing to do?'

→ Tackle your to-do list one item at a time: it's much more efficient to do things sequentially rather than simultaneously. Start with something that feels less easy than the rest, and you'll feel less overwhelmed when it's done.

→ You can survive for weeks without eating, but your head is wired up to enjoy the taste of high-energy, fatty foods. This was very helpful as we evolved in a hunter-gatherer lifestyle. It could be seen as a disadvantage in a world where you're normally within a five-minute drive of a McFlurry. Our brains have evolved to survive starvation, not to resist plenty; regardless of what your primitive instincts try to tell you, waiting a little longer will not be fatal.

→ Use the same principle to prioritize what to put in your rucksack, pockets, car glovebox or bag using PLAN. Rather than wasting your phone's valuable battery life on the torch function as you walk back from the pub down dark streets, clip a tiny LED torch onto your keyring.

→ Get some first-aid training and carry a first-aid kit that you're familiar with in your car or backpack. You never know; one day you may be able to save the life of someone you love.

We've now covered one corner of the Survival Triangle – PLAN. The next side we'll look at is Work. How do some people push themselves so much harder and further than others, and how can we learn to do the same?

Chapter 3

GETTING THINGS DONE
HOW TO WORK EFFICIENTLY

One misty autumnal dawn in the Rocky Mountains of 1808, near present-day Three Forks, Montana, two explorers and trappers were canoeing along a river when they heard an unusual rumbling. John Potts thought it was the sound of buffalo, the other trapper John Colter thought it was Indians. Colter suggested they leave the area and inspect the rest of their traps the next day. Potts was convinced it was buffalo and persuaded him to continue.

The high value of beaver pelts at the time led Colter and Potts to go trapping for them in a high-risk region, territory dominated by the Blackfeet tribe. After several recent deadly encounters, including one where John Colter himself had fought and was wounded alongside the Flathead and Crow people – enemies of the Blackfeet – the Blackfeet had come to regard all white men as hostile. Colter and Potts knew that, so, in order to avoid detection, they were setting their traps under the cover of night and collecting them at first light, then laying-up out of sight all day. Now, just after first light, the strange rumbling noise had got louder.

As the pair silently rounded a corner in the river, hundreds of Blackfeet warriors, some armed with guns, appeared on its east bank. Colter surreptitiously slipped his metal traps over the side of his canoe; the river wasn't deep, the traps were valuable and incriminating, and he hoped to return and collect them in the future.

The Blackfeet's leader beckoned them over to the bank. Colter weighed up their options; it was impossible to make a clean getaway from their current position, it was also impossible to try to fight their way out from the river. With any immediate escape therefore ruled out, he paddled to the bank; Colter had travelled in the region for years and hoped that they may just be robbed and then released. Diplomacy may yet prevail.

Potts remained in his canoe in the centre of the stream, watching to see what happened to Colter. The answer came quickly; as soon as his canoe reached the bank Colter was seized, disarmed and stripped naked. He understood some native languages but not the Blackfeet's, but even so it was obvious that they wanted Potts to come over too. So he called to Potts, who replied from the centre of the stream that he'd rather die quickly there, than be stripped, robbed and then murdered. At this obvious defiance, one of the Blackfeet shot at Potts, knocking him down in his canoe and wounding his hip.

'Are you hurt?' shouted Colter.

'Yes,' replied Potts. 'Too hurt to escape; if you can get away, do it. I'll kill at least one of them.' As he said that he rose up from the bottom of his canoe, levelled his rifle and fired at the Blackfeet, hitting and killing one of them. Before the grey smoke of that shot had cleared, hundreds of bullets and arrows were heading towards Potts, instantly riddling both him and his craft.

Warriors then surged into the river and hauled Potts' body to the shore, brutally dismembering it with their axes and hurling his organs and entrails at Colter. Worse still, enraged relatives of the man Potts had shot tried to hack at Colter with tomahawks and were only just kept at bay by other Blackfeet. Colter knew his life was likely to be painfully snuffed out at any second.

Standing naked and with his companion's blood running down his skin, Colter watched as the group's leader made his decision. He stood there, fully expecting pain and death; a blow from a tomahawk, a knife, who knew what. Abruptly, the chief pointed towards the open prairie. It stretched out in front of him for miles; flat, rocky and strewn with thorny prickly pear cacti. Unsure what was happening, Colter didn't move. Another, older member of the group motioned urgently to Colter to get going. So he started to walk, naked, onto the prairie, the old man becoming more urgent and emphatic in his gestures until Colter picked up his pace a little. Colter expected to feel the sharp heat of a shot or spear in his exposed back at any moment, thinking he was being told to move to make him a clearer target. When he was about eighty metres away he looked round and saw the younger warriors hurriedly taking off their leggings and other cumbersome items.

The penny dropped; it was to be a race, and his scalp was the prize. Colter set off running as fast as he could. He was a very fit man, renowned for his endurance and athleticism. Now, those qualities were put to the ultimate test. He ran and ran, the many thorns and sharp rocks under his bare feet were the least of his worries. His chest heaved in oxygen and his nose began to bleed with the exertion, spattering his chin and chest red.

After he'd been running for a while he dared to briefly look back. He saw that he was making great ground; only one warrior was clear of the pack and keeping pace with him. He might get away if he could just deal with this one Blackfoot who was way ahead of all the others. So Colter stopped, and the front-runner rapidly approached with his spear in his right hand and thin blanket streaming from his left shoulder. Colter shouted an appeal to him in the Crow language, but the warrior just fixed both hands on his spear and, without slowing, charged ahead at the naked, blood-smeared prize.

As the final metre between them closed, John Colter dodged to one side and grabbed the warrior's spear behind its point. Using the brave's momentum against him, he twisted and knocked him onto the ground. The force of the effort snapped the spearhead off in Colter's hand, and he immediately thrust it into the chest of the prone, disarmed attacker. Quickly withdrawing the blade from its now dying former owner, he grabbed the discarded blanket and ran on across the plain.

Colter pointed himself at the nearest fork in the Madison River, as he could make out its tree-lined banks in the distance. He knew the geography of the area from all of his previous explorations, and as he ran the river was getting nearer with every painful stride. With his recently obtained cutting tool and blanket, his ultimate survival prospects had risen above zero for the first time since Potts's death.

Soon he heard the chasing pack let up a chilling yell as they reached the spot of his brief fight with their dead comrade, but by now Colter's five-mile dash to the river was over. He dived into its deep waters and struck out towards a ten-foot-high pile of tangled logs and dead branches that were breaking the surface nearby. Recognizing it as a beaver lodge, Colter ducked under the river's surface and found the lodge's submerged entrance. He crawled in and upwards, to the air chamber and platform inside, and hid there as his hunters arrived.

We know where Colter hid from a man called Thomas James, who actually retraced Colter's route with him much later. Other accounts describe rafts of driftwood, but hiding under that would have meant enduring hours of prolonged immersion in cold river water, and that would have been physiologically impossible for any human.

After reaching the water, the Blackfeet warriors scoured up and down both banks for hours, at times standing on top of Colter's hide-site. He thought they might try to burn or dig him out, but it looks like by finding that beaver lodge he'd stumbled upon the only place no one else could conceive of as somewhere for a human to hide.

When night fell, he emerged via the underwater entrance and swam downstream to make some distance towards safety. His survival trek would ultimately take him across a high mountain pass to friendly territory, which lay over 200 miles distant. During that autumn evasion through the Rockies, Colter only had his previous experiences, a blanket and a spear tip to help him. His vast local knowledge acquired over many years was the key to his success, allowing him to use his two meagre items to survive the cold, high mountains and then to subsist on carbohydrate-rich plant roots on the plains. Colter finally arrived as an unrecognizably gaunt shadow at the remote outpost of Fort Raymond, eleven days after his escape run had begun.

It's an awe-inspiring feat – evading naked through hostile mountainous territory. As a stripped-down test of one person's ability to keep going with only their skills and knowledge, it's hard to beat.

We can see some parallels with other stories we've looked

at so far here: the importance of relevant experience and flexibility, the articulation of very clear goals. But at the core of this story is an incredible act of mental and physical stamina. The key to Colter's survival was that he just kept going.

Pain management

In our everyday lives, it's unlikely that we'll be called upon to test ourselves in quite the same way that Colter was. But we all face moments in our lives when we can either keep going or give up. Some people seem to have that ineffable quality and some just don't; this is what the researcher Angela Duckworth has called 'grit'[12] and characterizes as 'perseverance and passion for very long-term goals'. Importantly, the people she tends to study are those that put themselves in situations deliberately, whereas we're looking at what gets people through unexpected events. However, there are interesting areas of overlap, and there are techniques that I know of which we can use to cultivate perseverance in adversity whether we chose to be there or not.

In all of our lives, there will be times when we feel stuck in the middle of a slog. Whether it's a difficult project, or a particularly fractious meeting, there are times when we all have to grit our teeth and dig in.

No pain, no gain

Studies have shown that the best endurance athletes don't feel less pain than us, they are just better practised at managing it. Their techniques for managing exertion pain are similar to John Colter's, and learnable by us all. In a study of Olympic cyclists, it was found that they performed best not if they tried to distract themselves by thinking of some kind of pain-free 'happy place', but instead by focusing their mental energy on the activity they were doing, in their case the precise motion of efficient pedalling. 'Your mind cannot be elsewhere. That's the thing. You need to be focused on the moment.'[13] As was the case for John Colter, top-level athletes all have a keen awareness of their bodies, an understanding of its limitations and an ability to keep going.

The study also found that pain management was assisted by preparing a plan and sticking to it, even if its goal was distant – in their case the Olympics, in John Colter's case getting away from the people chasing him. Knowing what to expect, and that ultimately there will be respite, whether that's reaching the top of a long hill climb on a bike or just stopping to rest with the beavers, allows the present pain to be accepted en route to a goal. Achieving the goal is elevated above the distraction of any pain, turning down the volume of discomfort.

Most of us would rightfully feel that our lives are more complicated than a simple foot race to freedom. But if we actually took the time to write down what our longest-term goals are, we'd see that ultimately we can find a way of making them join up with what we're doing now. Crucial to our ability to keep going is to articulate these long-term goals and focus on them when we're mired in the hardship of specific tasks. Being able to take a step back, to get perspective on how this moment relates to our largest goals, allows us to keep going through that hardship. The key is to start to articulate it to yourself.

You can try this yourself when faced with something that feels insurmountable – even if it's not your 'out loud voice'. The cyclists would use something like, 'I've prepared myself; I can get through this. It will get easier soon. Everybody else [in the race] is suffering too.' Just as with other situations we've looked at, endurance athletes found that focused or relaxed breathing is one of the best techniques for achieving performance efficiency, stress reduction and also pain management. People think they will either cope or they won't because of how they were born. Not true.

You can train your brain to deal with suffering and discomfort, just like you can train your body.

The first step is to recognize the suffering, not ignore it, and then to frame it in your own terms. As with other things, it can be useful to make a note of situations when you can feel yourself suffering at a task – take a moment to recognize the suffering and note down what might be making you feel it. If you do this often enough, you'll come up with your own set of personalized performance markers. Just as a professional athlete comes to know how long they can operate at 100 per cent, you need to know what your capabilities are and recognize what impacts them.

Your personal limits may be a blend of the physical and psychological redlines. In times of pressure, it's useful to know what to do to counter these potential blows, and how to delay or avoid their effects. If you know something is likely to adversely affect you, remember that you can train yourself to cope with it better. For instance, one of the toughest people I knew when we were learning to fly was broken during our life raft training in the English Channel, completely debilitated both physically and emotionally by seasickness.* It was a powerful visual lesson for me. Not only in how everyone has vulnerabilities, but also that we should always carry anti-seasickness tablets, and in how prevalent diced carrot is as an ingredient.

Don't ignore your limits

The first thing you need to do is to recognize that you have limits. The people that get themselves into the worst difficulties when we're training are the ones who think they're

---

* Unavailable to us back then during our training drill, the best cure for seasickness is to sit under a tree.

superheroes. They think they can run at full speed, not stop for breaks, not eat, not sleep and their performance is somehow still going to keep at maximum. As we touched upon with Dale Zelko's story earlier, you can't negotiate with your physical needs indefinitely. You can stretch your performance and needs for a while but they're eventually going to snap back with a vengeance.

What we'll look at now is how to use this idea to identify our own potential physiological weak spots. When we're physically and mentally tired, we're not making the best decisions. Let's deal with the simple things first and then move on to the bigger stuff.

What simple things stop us getting things done?

Lack of sleep

A pretty constant theme in the survival stories I've studied is the need for proper rest. It's impossible to keep going indefinitely, and a natural response to coming down off any huge spike in stress is a feeling of fatigue. Our brains need a break from high-stakes challenges and the best break is sleep. In his recent book *Why We Sleep*, the neuroscientist Matthew Walker makes a convincing case for sleep being one of the most important factors in our physical and mental well-being, finding that, among other things:

- An afternoon nap increases the brain's learning capacity by 15–20 per cent
- Sleep improves your memory, reducing things forgotten by 30–50 per cent
- A good night's sleep improves time to physical exhaustion when exercising by 10–30 per cent

I know when I haven't had enough sleep, my brain starts to make the daftest mistakes. It was one of the earliest of my physical boundaries I ever hit when I joined the RAF; I was out on my first escape and evasion exercise when I was so fatigued several nights in that I hallucinated a cartoon wasp. I stood, fascinated, watching it as I fell asleep standing, and then faceplanted onto the ground. Ultimately, sleep deprivation is potentially lethal. When we're tired, it can become harder to fight off the shortcuts our brain wants to take, as we are lacking in processing power.

I've now taken to following survival best practice and getting in the odd power nap. The sort of strategies you'll take to plan and prioritize should mean fewer distractions cycling round in your brain when you try to go to sleep. It's the foundation that everything else builds upon, so try and put some time into getting more of it. If you'd like a quick fix to sleep better at night, don't charge your phone next to your bed. It's daylight-blue toned screen is giving your brain jet lag and being constantly connected is tiring in itself.[14]

Temperature

Our evolution in Africa means that our bodies are tuned to operate, naked, in an environment that's between 26°C and 30°C. The figure varies slightly from person to person, but that's our species' benchmark. It's called our thermoneutral temperature, and it is the sweet spot between higher and lower still-air temperatures that can make us sweat or shiver, both of which use up valuable resources. In this ideal zone, our skin temperature is around 33°C, our body core temperature is 37°C, and this key figure is maintained by adjusting the amount of warm blood we push towards the skin.

So when it gets warmer we push more blood to the skin's surface, vasodilating to cool down, and when it gets cooler we stop, vasoconstricting to conserve warmth. If our environment gets any warmer than 30°C, this trick isn't enough, and we'll start to sweat too. If it gets any cooler than 26°C we may start to shiver. This is our thermoregulatory zone – your body's engine is actively having to do something to keep you at the right temperature, and that uses more fuel.

If you're hot and take no steps to cool down, this will leave you feeling irritable, your ability to make good decisions will be impaired along with your physical performance, and all the sweating will lead to muscle cramps. If you still don't get cooler the condition will get worse fast; as your body temperature rises you will develop a life-threatening heatstroke, where a victim normally stops sweating and has hot, dry skin. If nothing is done for them this will lead to unconsciousness, brain damage and death.

If I'm about to do something that needs brain power, I take a moment to check if I'm too hot or too cold. There's no point not taking care of that before you begin. If you've ever experienced how poorly you make decisions when rushing to meet friends on a hot summer's day, you'll know how quickly an increase in temperature can impact your decision-making. Just take a moment to check, take a layer on or off, open or close a window. Job done.

Thirst

We've already seen that as little as 1 per cent dehydration can lead to mental impairment. Offices often work very hard to make sure that drinks are available but people don't realize just how much and how frequently they should be drinking to keep at optimal hydration. To gauge how dehydrated you are day to day, the simplest indicator is the colour of your urine. Clear is best, straw-coloured is good, the darker after that the worse it is. You should drink enough water to aim for at least one clear pee a day, wherever you may be. So, as far as hydration is concerned, the only real-life survival use for your urine is recognizing and monitoring how dehydrated you actually are, whatever you might see on the TV.

What I tend to do is try and drink one glass of water every time I stop for a break, which works out as roughly eight glasses a day. And it doesn't need to be straight old water – a warm caffeinated cuppa has more than just hydration to offer. Caffeine is the drug of choice if you want to help your brain to pay attention, and drinking tea or coffee won't dehydrate you as is sometimes said – there's just too much water in the cup for that. If you have to choose, go for tea. As well as caffeine, it also contains a substance called L-Theanine, which makes tea's caffeine boost more gradual and longer-lasting than the short spike you get from L-Theanine-free coffee.

Not taking breaks

However motivated you are, you won't be able to work flat out indefinitely. Even Colter had to take a break. I've found that I can't really keep going on a task that requires total mental focus for more than ninety minutes without my concentration flagging.

After that, physical and mental tiredness mean that you're less able to make good decisions. You might find everything feels too much, or that you're drawn to faffing with smaller jobs that don't really improve your situation. When that happens, get up from what you're doing and stretch your legs. Have a brew or drink some more water.

Lack of personalization

Always try and make sure you visualize the result of completing a task. It's much easier to pick up sticks if you're thinking about the warm fire and cooked food that will come from it. What you need to do is convince your brain that the effort is worth the reward. Some words on paper and an abstract concept won't always do it, but re-weighting the task so you can show the actual reward might do.

Self-bribe

When all else fails, self-bribe. Any hiker who's ever been cold and miserable knows the benefit of promising themselves a square of chocolate or Kendal Mint Cake when they reach a waypoint. Do the same with your survival task list. Don't be afraid of giving yourself external rewards if you can't make internal ones work for you.

The importance of treats

Salvador Alvarenga spent 438 days drifting across the Pacific Ocean when his fishing trip from Mexico went wrong in

2012. Of the many horrors he endured, thirst was almost constant, especially if the rains failed. As he neared the Marshall Islands after drifting for over 6,000 miles in his small, powerless boat – unknowingly towards the end of his epic journey as the world's longest-ever documented sea-survivor – plastic bottles with a strange brown liquid at the bottom began to drift past in the current. By this stage – it was now 2014 – he'd become an expert oceanic scavenger who would seek out any opportunity for rewards, so he collected the bottles and cautiously sipped the brown fluid, which also seemed to contain wood shavings. It tasted peppery but drinkable; it numbed his dry tongue but as it did so he felt a surge of energy. The bottles were something to savour. It was only after he'd made landfall on Ebon Atoll and been found by locals that he discovered what the mystery energy drink was. The locals chew a small betel nut and spit the dark fluid it generates into bottles. When he worked this link out Alvarenga gagged, but while he'd been at sea, drinking the contents of disposable spittoons had been a treat. I remember this story, because it shows that it always pays to find treats where you can. When I've been slogging through deep arctic snow to build a smoke-generating signal fire, I reward myself when it's done with one of the small 'emergency-ration' candies; try and make any rewards deliberate and part of your motivation.

Distraction

Wherever we spend our time these days, our general connectivity means that we are far more likely to be distracted from any tasks that need concentration. Your thinking power will be even more fragile if you're tired, thirsty and hungry in remote wilderness.

Even on a very small scale, if you are trying to get something done that requires focus, interruptions can be really costly to your effectiveness. Real-world studies have shown that if you are fully focused on a task and somebody 'pops in for a quick chat' or says 'have you got a moment?', then your train of thought gets disrupted. And if that happens it will take you on average twenty minutes to get back to the point of focus that your thoughts were at before your creative spell was broken.[15]

If you're trying to solve a life or death problem outdoors (the classic example here is fixing a radio), your concentration can even be broken by a sudden change in the weather. The best survival shelters always include enough extra small space to allow you to work on these kinds of tasks as well as rest. More likely and equally as risky, if you get distracted during any job that you're doing as part of your PLAN, you can misplace vital equipment. So, avert potential disaster and have a system for where you keep any survival tools, and even better, tie these items onto your person.

I imagine some of you reading this book are toying with

the idea of entering a survival TV arena like the show *Alone*. A great example of the price of losing a key bit of gear is in episode one of season seven of *Alone* where a contestant misplaces his ferro-rod after making a great start in the Arctic; that episode was titled 'Million Dollar Mistake.' Wherever you are, if you work with constant interruptions then you can never fully focus, which makes it hard to do the tasks on your list that require that kind of immersive attention.

Practising everyday evasion

As a survival instructor who loves being outdoors, I try to avoid time behind my desk as much as possible. If you need to avoid being interrupted by someone trying to track you down, sometimes you need to get a little more inventive. This is where you can employ some of the skills of the poacher. If you need to go off grid for an hour or two but you need your family or colleagues to think you are still somewhere in the building, you can adapt the military's well-loved 'two hat' anti-tracking ruse.

In armies, navies and air forces around the world, personnel have to wear appropriate headgear when they're outdoors. To prevent the sky falling in. Some of us have used this to our advantage for years. It follows then, that if I need to leave the building I must wear my beret. I make sure that when I'm in the building, my beret is always hung on the wall in a prominent but not overly obvious spot. If when I leave the building it must be on my head, then it also follows that its small patch of office wall space must be empty if I'm outside the building. So when I'm leaving in 'poacher mode', to do something uninterrupted elsewhere, I bring my spare 'stunt beret' out of my bottom drawer, and hang it on the wall. Once I've slipped out of the building wearing my actual beret, any would-be office trackers will initially look for me at my desk.

They see the stunt beret and 'he's in the building' is their first and final thought. I get a lot more time to practice my survival skills these days. Try it with a spare jacket or bag. You're welcome.

Fire discipline

Distractions aside, getting things done can also hinge on our ability to use our resources effectively. Fire is one such resource. It transcends the priorities of survival, the elements of PLAN; you can protect yourself with it, get rescued because of it and it can make water and food safe to consume. But to the unwary, there can be a tipping point where the fire stops working for them and it becomes a distraction in and of itself. If you're using it inefficiently, it can take up huge amounts of time gathering firewood to satiate the fire's growing appetite. So always use fire as a tool, make it do what you need when you want it done, rather than having it constantly stoked up.

While out in the wilderness, try to have your meals or warm drinks at a set time of day. Last light is good because then you can use the fire's glow to work by while it is simultaneously cooking your food; its smoke is also deterring to no-see-ums and mosquitoes. If you can batch tasks that require fire together in this way, you'll use a lot less firewood, and burn far less of your valuable time and energy too.

Keep moving

Not many of us would fancy a five-mile sprint like John Colter, but getting some exercise is absolutely essential. Modern patterns of work are causing increasing numbers of us to spend huge portions of our lives sitting down, a fact that researches have linked to the rise in obesity, type 2 diabetes and even some types of cancer.[16] But illness risks aside, there are survival benefits to staying active, like better sleep, increased energy and improved brain power.

The basic rule is that you should try and include some medium-intensity exercise in your day. A really simple real-world hack is to take the stairs for anything below five flights. It's like doing a bit of survival fitness conditioning by stealth rather than having to make time to hit a treadmill.

An added bonus is that the more you exercise, the easier it should be for you to sleep. A short walk will boost the amount of blood that pumps to all your major organs, including your brain, and making walking a regular habit will also increase the neural connections between your brain cells. In survival, this can simply be the walk you take each day to check any traps that you have put out. The science is that because you are moving, some of your brain power is being used to control that movement, meaning it isn't focused on suppressing mental distractions, which is part of the reason why walking has been shown to increase creative thought. Fresh ideas and insights are freer to bubble up to the surface. The speed that you walk is important too; if you try to go too quickly, that in itself uses up the spare mental capacity that you need to generate your next big idea, too slowly and the really creative thoughts may not emerge.

Notable walkers include Charles Darwin and William Wordsworth, and the more contemporary Nobel Prize-winning psychologist Daniel Kahneman, renowned for his work on 'fast' and 'slow' decision-making, who does some of his best thinking while walking. He's even measured the exact speed that works for him: a mile in seventeen minutes, best described as a stroll.* So the next time you need to get

* Ironically, sort of in between walking fast and slow.

inventive, go for a short stroll. This regular practice helps generate creative responses to all manner of life's problems.

Extreme motivation

We've now looked at quite a few useful ways of taking care of the controllable factors that can impinge on our ability to get things done. But what about the very biggest feats of endurance? What can we do to ensure we're best set up to replicate those?

These are the main physiological levers that we can move, to make sure we're giving ourselves the best chance of concentrating, but what about the psychological aspects? What about those people who seem capable of extraordinary feats of endurance? What can we learn from them?

I'd like to tell you the story of one man who I think best exemplifies the extraordinary mental aspects of the survival mindset. In SERE circles, what Lance Sijan managed to endure, both physically and mentally, is legendary. The true definition of indomitable, here's the story of what he did; it's to my mind the best example of an unconquerable spirit in modern survival history. And it helps us to begin to understand the most often missing piece of the motivation puzzle.

Lance Sijan

Lance Sijan was a US Air Force pilot whose aircraft was blown up on a bombing run over the Laotian jungle on 9 November 1967, in the height of the Vietnam War.

After falling through the trees from his exploding jet and losing consciousness, he awoke to see his numb left leg flopping at a weird angle, bone protruding through the skin. His right hand was smashed up – three of the fingers dislocated into bad angles too – and his arm was sticky with blood from deep cuts. The force of it all had removed his flying helmet, and as he gingerly touched the matted blood in his hair he also felt a softer, yielding patch of his skull behind his left ear.

His injuries looked sickening and made him gag, but he knew enough first aid to realize that he was lucky. His head injury was bad – he was concussed – but his skull wasn't fractured badly enough to kill him. Similarly, as he managed to use some of his medical kit to dress his leg wound, he saw that although his left leg was flopping below the knee, he was lucky that the sharp protruding bone hadn't severed an artery, or he'd have already bled out. Then, with intense pain starting to come in spasms, he bound up the leg, drank some water, injected one of his morphine syringes and passed out.

Thirty-six hours after his jet had evaporated beneath him, he was conscious again. Holding his survival radio to his face, he leaned back against the buttress root of a giant jungle hardwood tree and radioed for rescue.

Over the next two days an aerial armada of over one hundred US aircraft tried in vain to pluck Lance from his karst hillside. North Vietnamese Army anti-aircraft fire held them at bay and even shot down one of the would-be rescuers. The pick-up had to be called off when Lance was no longer able to communicate. Unbeknown to the task force above him, he'd fallen into a hole in the limestone the day before – while crawling backwards to reach a rescue hoist – and hit his already fractured skull. He'd been knocked out doing so and the battery on his radio had slowly died as he lay there. He flickered in and out of consciousness over the next day, lying in the small sinkhole. Once he eventually regained full consciousness – and he realized what had happened to his now severed radio lifeline – his ordeal really began.

Everything is harder if you're injured and in pain. Lance was determined not to be captured but he knew he was surrounded by enemy troops on his limestone mountaintop; he'd heard their patrols communicating with whistles close by during the first day of the rescue attempt. Looking up, he could see that the jungle he was in was dense – it had three layers of canopy towering above him, as he lay way below in the leaf litter. He knew he couldn't communicate with friendlies by radio now as his battery was too weak, and that the jungle was too thick where he was to attract their attention visually. So, he formed a plan: evade to a better location, away from the enemy troops, where he could attract the attention of friendly aircraft with his signal mirror.

The soil was thin on the karst, but the forest floor was still alive with a universe of flies, crawling insects and blood-sucking leeches. His only way of moving was by lying on his back and pushing himself with his good right leg. This was how he had to evade. Head first, backwards, over sharp, jagged outcrops of limestone, while trying to protect his battered leg, arm, hand and skull. He did that for *over a month*.

So, how can anyone motivate themselves to do that; how does anyone endure that kind of prolonged pain, in an already oppressive environment? For me, this goes beyond Colter to another level. The carrots and sticks for Lance – the psychological hooks that his motivation hung from – were varied, but importantly he was fully aware of the even grimmer reality of capture. Like Colter, he knew clearly what the downside of stopping would be. He'd seen American pilots who'd been paraded by the North Vietnamese on TV. They'd looked broken and brainwashed, making statements under duress admitting to crimes they'd not committed. He also knew that his chances of staying alive in captivity long enough to reach any indoctrination camp were slim; many enemy troops must have been killed by the prolonged bombing in support of the earlier attempts to rescue him. If he were taken, his immediate captors were sure to seek brutal revenge upon him for their killed and maimed comrades. Lance had already stated many times that he would do anything to avoid capture – giving himself up was definitely not an option. Likewise, if he stayed where he was he couldn't get rescued; therefore if he didn't move he would eventually die. To survive, he simply had to move.

But an even more important part of Lance's motivation to evade capture came from the close ties he had with his family. The carrot, rather than the stick. From all of the evidence I've seen, strong family bonds are a key source of mental strength which people draw on in order to endure hardships. In his room at Da Nang Air Base he had a collection of photos of his mother, father, brother and sister – at their home in Milwaukee – that he would stand and contemplate before leaving for each mission. He was also fiercely proud of his country and his service.

Perhaps most importantly, he'd gradually fallen in love with one of the flight attendants that had brought him into theatre three months previously. He had managed to arrange meetups with Lenora several times since, by volunteering to ferry squadron jets due for servicing back south whenever she was in country on another Continental Airlines trip. They'd spent several intense short breaks together this way, where they had built up a very strong bond, even starting to plan for a married life together in a hope-filled, post-war future.

When he set off from the karst, Lance didn't know how long it would take until he reached an area that was suited to visual signalling. He had an evasion map of the whole region, but that didn't have the kind of detail needed to work out exactly where to aim for. So he made his evasion goal simple; get off the steep, wooded, jagged limestone hillside and onto the more open lower valley. During the failed rescue attempts he'd heard the friendly aircraft and the enemy guns, so he knew the land eastwards would be best suited for a future pick-up attempt, lowering the chances of enemy interference. Lance had successfully established situational awareness and an achievable goal, now all he had to do was endure pain, and he knew he could do that.

It's also important to know here that Lance had played a lot of contact sport when he was younger, and he'd been through other tough physical training, including a jungle survival course before Vietnam. The hard knocks he'd had over the years helped him now. He compared the task ahead to his previous experience in terms of physical pain – measured it against what he knew he'd already pushed through in the past – and decided to try. As with the professional athletes discussed earlier, he was able to compare the suffering he was experiencing to some frame of reference. No football match or jungle survival course will ever put you into the deepest gullies of pain that he was in, but having experienced some of what he was about to face, he knew he could attempt more. So he started moving towards his goal – one heel push at a time.

Lance managed his pain, including severe dehydration and lack of food, and evaded on his back until Christmas Day 1967. He'd been blown up on the ninth of November. All he'd eaten in that time was some foliage and a few leeches, and although he'd been on his back he was still using energy as he crawled through the jungle. His clothes were as shredded as his body was. His plan had always been to reach an open area and contact friendly aircraft from there. He was going to do this with his signal mirror, so he would need an open area with full sun. Luckily, by day the enemy stayed out of open areas, because they were easier targets for American bombers if they stepped out from under the jungle canopy.

Lance had no accurate idea of the date by this point – his watch had been broken by the explosion, and was frozen at 8.39 – but he'd been able to guess at roughly how long he'd been going once he cleared the jungle canopy and saw the moon's phase. So he didn't know that it was Christmas Day as he lay in the open, or that the North Vietnamese were making the most of a twenty-four-hour Christmas ceasefire and bombing halt to move as many troops as they could in daylight. He'd been evading for forty-six days when a truck convoy of enemy reinforcements almost ran him over. He was bundled into the truck; captured.

Even after he was captured, and by now an emaciated wreck, he didn't lose his motivation to get home. He actually managed to escape, karate chopping a guard who he'd lured close and stealing his rifle. But while his mind was unbroken, his body was in a pitiful state; he crawled slowly away from the hut on his back during a tropical downpour. He was free again for a few hours. After recapture his treatment was sadistically cruel – he was denied any medical treatment and repeatedly beaten on his terrible wounds.

He was moved to other holding camps and eventually held with other Americans, one who'd known him before. Guy Gruters had been Lance's friend through training and had been on the parachute display team with him, but at first he couldn't recognize the physical wreck he encountered. He did recognize his spirit though; Lance had always been determined. Now, even though his hip bones were protruding through his skin, he was talking of trying to escape. The beatings, lack of medical treatment and terrible sanitary conditions of the camps, coupled with Lance's now-infected injuries, meant that he began to lapse into delirium and unconsciousness more frequently. Lance finally succumbed physically to pneumonia, but even when he was at death's door his spirit was unbroken, his determination to escape remained. He died on 22 January 1968.

The importance of belonging

What I take away from this story most, after the extraordinary bravery and physical and mental resilience that Lance Sijan displayed, is how determined we can be when our short-term targets and our most deeply held long-term goals are aligned. We all know the hoary old phrase 'find something you love and you'll never work a day in your life', but there is something in it.

So far we've explored the importance of articulating specific, achievable goals so that we can enjoy the virtuous circle of achieving them. This is because in survival contexts, our most important long-term goal is pretty clear and pretty easy to understand. To be rescued, live and return to the people and lives that we love.

However, in our daily lives, often our long-term goals are much more obliquely related to our everyday tasks, and can be multiple, overlapping and contradictory, which means that it can be hard to tap into that deepest layer of motivation. Sadly, for the majority of us, our working lives are not often about the constant articulation of our guiding passion, but something more complicated.

What we need to do is try and connect them up in some way, to get the benefit of that psychological effect. After all, we don't need to crawl backwards with broken limbs, we just need to be able to get that boring bit of admin done.

However, the fundamental rule remains. If our own passion, our own sense of who we are and where we want to get to, is naturally aligned with the task in front of us and we can clearly understand how it moves us one step closer to our ultimate goals, then we can accomplish incredible things. I also think it's important that those goals are related to other people. Angela Duckworth reports that when she talks to what she calls 'grit paragons', often their goals are immediately related to other people, whether it's their direct family, or something more abstract, like their country or their sport.[17] Lance had both, but is there anything we can do in the way we frame tasks to remind ourselves that we are ultimately helping others by completing them? One of the things that the most successful companies are very good at doing is creating a sense of mission, so that those who work for them feel part of a shared, high-level goal, something that is changing the world.

Work out what you want and who you are

You need to complete the work on a presentation because your team needs it so that they can continue to get supported in their task. Of course, ultimately, if you do it well, this will benefit your standing within the company, but that's all quite diffuse and understandably your brain finds it hard to recognize where the urgent reward is in the normal way – it still wants to know why you should put yourself through this hardship to achieve it.

What you can do is to try and find things within a task that do tap into a passion of yours. Before I joined the RAF, I went to art school and art and design are still big parts of my life. I know that I'm far more likely to keep going on a mundane task if I can find some element within it that relates to this. So when I'm putting together slides for a lesson, I try and find the very best photographs that illustrate my point. If it's important to you to be kind, try thinking about how what you're doing ultimately benefits people. If you've always had an interest in performance, try thinking about how you can make your presentation as entertaining as it can be. An alternative would be to think about all of the rewards that completing the task brilliantly could unlock. See if you can find a way that it gets you closer to the very biggest things you want to do. It might be as simple as thinking how much better a partner or parent you'll be that weekend if you're not worrying about the task in front of you.

What we need to do is to find ways of connecting the tasks right in front of us with our longest-term goals, who we are and the things that are important to us. This will release the deepest well of motivation when we need to keep going. When I'm stuck in the middle of a seemingly unending admin task, which I can't summon up any passion for, I find it helps to think about what completing this task will unlock, how it will allow me to teach the instructors who will go on to teach thousands of men and women and ultimately make them more safe. At the heart of what I do is the satisfaction that comes from knowing if we get the small details right, then one day we could make a big difference.

After Guy Gruters and other prisoners were released five years later, they told of Lance Sijan's ordeal, in the jungle and the camps, of how his unconquerable spirit had been an inspiration and motivation for their own continued resistance. The US Air Force have recognized Lance's supreme example at their academy with a sculpture of his epic struggle on the jungle floor, helping to inspire future generations of their officers. Though he wasn't able to reach his loved ones, it is likely that his inspiration has ensured that many, many others have been able to.

Summary

→ Pain Management: remember the methods used by
  Olympic cyclists. Try to focus on the action you're doing

rather than the pain you're feeling, and know that there will be relief when you make it to your goal.

→ Have a word with yourself: without using your 'out loud' voice, remind yourself that you can do it. 'I've prepared myself; I can get through this. It will get easier soon. Everybody else in this meeting is suffering too.'

→ An understanding of heat illness symptoms will help you avoid it. If you're ever in a rush to meet your friends on a hot summer afternoon, knowing that being too hot can impair your decision-making should make you think twice before jumping onto the bus you just ran to without first checking that It's the right one.

→ To gauge how dehydrated you are day to day, the simplest indicator is the colour of your urine. Clear is best, straw-coloured is good, the darker after that the worse it is. You should drink enough water to aim for at least one clear pee a day, wherever you may be.

→ If you're really busy during a hot dry spell, the best way to avoid hyponatremia (having too little sodium) is to vary your fluid intake from just water, and include sweeter drinks and maybe a little salt on your chips to maintain your body's mineral balance.

→ Some stuff shouldn't be drunk, no matter what you see on screen. Drinking urine that is twice as salty as your body will kill you faster than not drinking it would have done. In the military, along with seawater, we teach people to never drink urine. Science shows that it's simply the wrong thing to do; you will survive for longer by drinking nothing than you will if you drink any salty water.

→ Have a cup of tea. It contains all the stuff your brain wants to help boost your mental performance. Learning how to brew-up in the great outdoors will build your self-reliance and therefore your self-confidence wherever you roam.

→ Evade distractions – it'll take you twenty minutes to get back on task if your train of thought is interrupted. Make your shelter big enough to fix small fiddly items of gear in, out of the distractions of bad weather. And if you don't want a costly repercussion from being distracted while you're outside, tie any vital bits of gear onto your person and have a set place for everything that's not in use.

→ Fresh ideas and insights are freer to bubble up to the surface when you go for a stroll. The speed that you walk is important; if you try to go too quickly, that in itself uses up the spare mental capacity that you need to generate your next big idea, too slowly and the really creative thoughts may not emerge.

Now we've explored the practical steps we can take to actually execute our plans, it's time to understand why that feeling of forward momentum is so important. It's time to look at another side of the Survival Triangle – the fundamental importance of hope.

Chapter 4

SMALL STEPS AND THE IMPORTANCE OF HOPE

In the middle of a small park just south of the River Thames in London is a beautiful white building. A blue-green copper dome rises above its colonnaded entrance. Once the site of the famous old Bethlem Royal Hospital, known colloquially as Bedlam, it is now the London home of the Imperial War Museum. Outside, mounted by the steps, they have a pair of fifteen-inch naval guns and inside they have a huge variety of military equipment, including tanks, submarines and fighter planes. If you go up the stairs and turn right, on the far side of the second floor is what looks like an old rowing boat. Most people walk right past it to look at the more glamorous stuff, but I can spend ages looking at this unassuming piece. If you look closely at the rim around the top of its hull, known as the gunwale, you'll see a series of twenty-four small notches carved into the wood. Here's how they got there.

The SS *Anglo Saxon* was a British merchant ship, steaming about 700 miles off the coast of the Azores on the dark night of 21 August 1940. Without any warning, she was hit at close range by shells from an unseen German ship, igniting the ammunition for her deck gun and killing most of the crew.

The radio room was destroyed before any distress call could be sent. As the SS *Anglo Saxon* burned, her surviving crew tried to lower lifeboats but were machine-gunned by the raider, which had now closed right in. On the far side of the *Anglo Saxon*, however, seven men had managed to escape in the ship's open 'jolly boat' without being seen, although three of them had been injured in the attack. They waited quietly in the dark as the raider finally moved off and their own ship sank, leaving no other survivors.

First Officer Barry C. Denny took charge of the little group, and at first was described as a 'tower of strength', getting the men into a daily routine, issuing their rations of half a dipper of water every morning and evening and half a biscuit at midday. He kept a log of events as they sailed westward by small compass under a blazing tropical sun, treating the injured and hoping to find land or be rescued by a ship. On the third night, they saw an unlit ship and prepared to signal to it with a sea flare. On closer inspection, though, they decided it was probably the raider, as they were only a hundred miles from where they sank, so they 'kept quiet and let her go off'.[18]

Several days were spent becalmed under the glare of the sun, its scattered rays reflecting harshly off the sea, with no rain to replenish their dwindling supplies of fresh water. The three men who'd been injured had by now received the last of the medical supplies and their wounded limbs were beginning to swell worryingly. Five days in, Denny wrote, 'Trusting to make a landfall in vicinity of Leeward Islands, with God's will and British determination.' As the rainless days wore on they grew weaker and skinnier, but spirits were still described by Denny as 'extremely cheerful'.

The next night, 30 August, a week into their ordeal, one of the injured men became delirious, keeping them awake all night with his moans.

His suffering continued for another two days until he finally died from blood poisoning on day eleven, 1 September. His body was cast overboard.

The next day, Denny's log, always understated, reads, 'Crew now feeling rather low'. It was the last entry he made; all subsequent notes were made in different handwriting.

The log entry on 3 September said, 'Things going from bad to worse, 1st mate [Denny] who wrote this diary up to this point going fast'.

On the fourth, the log notes that another man 'slipped overboard' – the truth was he actually climbed over the side intentionally and drowned. Survival had seemed impossible to him. The next day, Denny lost all hope and cracked, telling the other four, 'I'm going over the side, who's coming with me?' The engineer jumped too. On the ninth the cook died. He'd been drinking seawater – known by sailors for centuries to be a killer, Roy Widdicombe noting in the log, '2nd cook goes mad dies. Two of us left'.

Three days later, it started raining. Widdicombe's final log entry, on 24 September, simply states, 'All water and biscuits gone but still hoping to make land'.

Their ordeal would last until 30 October. By then, Robert Tapscott and Roy Widdicombe had travelled over 2,500 miles, arriving in the Bahamas after seventy days adrift, looking like sunburned skeletons. Roy had lost his front teeth from trying to eat his own shoes. They had broken open their compasses to drink the distilled water and alcohol within them. Of the seven who escaped the stricken *Anglo Saxon*, only one died of injuries. Had the three who climbed overboard stayed in the jolly boat, with its many day-marking notches, there's every chance they could've reached the Bahamas too.

There's always hope. So what happened? What happened to change Denny from that initial tower of strength to choosing to slip deliberately overboard? How can we approach difficult situations seemingly without end and keep going, so that we are still around to do the equivalent of making another notch on the gunwale? We've already seen that though you might not be to blame for the missile targeting your plane, or the shells blowing up your ship's boiler, you need to own what happens subsequently. Main-

taining control in adversity takes determination, perseverance and, most importantly, hope.

What happened to Denny is part of a phenomenon that
has been called 'Give-up-itis'. Sadly, even people who survive a potentially lethal event without suffering any injuries
can still die. Others within such people's groups have
described a gradual descent through a pattern of symptoms
until the brain goes into what is almost like a 'computer
shutdown' process. Once complete, this process ends in
death. What is perhaps more shocking is that this phenomenon is not uncommon, although it's not widely known
about outside of the survival instructor community. But it
also helps us understand how important hope is and how
its removal can be fatal.

One of the most powerful descriptions of this process
was written by Viktor Frankl, a psychiatrist who witnessed
it daily during his time as an inmate of Auschwitz. In that
extreme situation, here's what Viktor observed:

> A man who let himself decline because he could not
> see any future goal found himself occupied with
> retrospective thoughts . . . in robbing the present of its
> reality there lay a certain danger . . . everything in a
> way became pointless . . . Instead of taking the camp's
> difficulties as a test of their inner strength, they did not
> take their life seriously and despised it as something of
> no consequence. They preferred to close their eyes and

to live in the past. Life for such people became meaningless.[19]

In this most extreme of human experiences, we find one of the key pillars of the survival mindset – without some sense of a future goal and a sense that we can influence getting there, life becomes of no consequence and hope is impossible. This is because of how important having a feeling of control is in your life.

When I was learning to fly, there was a very deliberate way of taking over as the 'handling pilot' – the person in control. To hand over the aircraft, the instructor flying says to their student 'you have control'. You put your hands on the stick and power controls, your feet on the pedals, start flying the aircraft, and then say, 'I have control'. The instructor says 'you have control' again and takes their hands and feet off. Now the aircraft is all yours.

Unless you deliberately take control of a situation, the situation is flying your life, not you. You need to put your hands back on the controls – acknowledge to yourself that you're in charge of your flightpath – and keep them there. But equally you need to be aware of the pressures that ownership and leadership brings. Once you've taken the controls, what then?

Studies by survival psychologists like John Leach have shown that people who cope well with the impact phase of their life-changing event tend to cope better with the all-important 'recoil' phase which follows on immediately afterwards. This is a roughly three-hour to three-day window during which there's a gradual return of reasoning abilities – once the survivor's brain begins to adjust to their new situation – and the reality of what's just taken place sinks in. If this adjustment doesn't happen then there is the potential to go down a slippery slope of not coping well, which can culminate, in extreme cases, with complete psychological collapse; as we just saw in the case of the survivors from the SS *Anglo Saxon*, who perished before the jolly boat reached the Bahamas.

The psychological aspects of recoil can be made even harder to overcome when any of these factors are present: injury, fatigue, hypothermia, thirst, or hunger.

One crucial factor in the jolly boat was sleep deprivation, the influence of which was examined in Chapter 3. Sleep deprivation can be a very quick way to disrupt mental processes and undermine group morale, and sleeping in their tiny boat was hard enough already. This was quickly followed by the death of one of the crew from blood poisoning. This was a severe blow to the remaining crew's morale – he was the first of their band to die and it dramatically illustrated to them the knife-edge of their existence. Then there would have been the awareness that reaching land at the Leeward Islands wasn't necessarily a done deal.

I think it's likely that his death would have triggered feelings of guilt in the group's leader, Denny, as he would doubtless have felt responsible for the others and that he'd somehow failed to save one of them. Very quickly the narrative would have shifted from Denny being the leader of a group of men who were going to be rescued, by achieving the first goal they had set, to one in which they were all going to die with nothing to aim for and no achievable tasks. Denny is another example of what can happen when we don't shift mindset under pressure. If we maintain an old narrative when the context has changed, it's impossible to set achievable goals and therefore impossible to feel hope. What was worse was that he articulated that there was no hope and took more crew with him when he went over the edge. It would be hard to find a purer case study of the importance and difficulty of leadership under pressure and how the delicate chemistry of a group under stress can go quickly wrong.

Achievable goals

When we're faced with a task, we need to understand why we're doing what we're doing, how it leads to the shared goal and how we're going to be able to achieve that goal. For Denny, when you took away the shared goal of getting all the men to safety, he was unable to move his goal to 'getting as many of the men as possible to safety'. Suddenly any sense of shared purpose, in which the things he was doing would lead to success, fell away, and he lost all hope.

The pattern of psychological deterioration usually followed during recoil is reasoning, dependency, denial, with-drawal, apathy, and then potentially death. The answer is to do something. It's that simple. Humans are much simpler than we often think.

Doing pretty much anything, provided it's ultimately constructive, will help. Anyone who's ever had bad news and instinctively made a cup of tea will know this to be true. It's partly because of the comfort of the warmth and caffeine and sugar hit. But it's also that this tiny accomplishable task is something to cling to. Time and time again we find that those who survive have something they are doing every day, something that may ultimately be meaningless but which gives them a sense of purpose and progression. It can be as simple as checking and ordering provisions. As the two men who lasted the longest found, even the act of marking time gives a basic sense of headway. This will make the person who is struggling feel useful and regain a little control of their destiny. At sea, where job options are much more limited, untangling the rescue line – a long cord that's fitted to most lifeboats and rafts, with a small 'lifering' or quoit at one end – then stowing it ready for a 'man over-board' use is helpful and occupies time.

In the case of the jolly boat, I think the act of writing the log, which might seem superficial, was key, as it offered structure – it was a link back to the order of the recent past and it carried within it the hope that it would be read by someone in the future. Once Denny was unmoored from that, he began to descend into apathy.

Now, it's unlikely that we'll ever find ourselves in a jolly boat like Denny. But if we ever find ourselves in a situation that's gone bad when others are looking to us for leadership then we should think about those notches in the gunwale and what they represent.

On land, we can apply some of the same advice to difficult situations. If you're not going to make it all the way to your planned destination before dark, then you need to work out quickly what your next best place to stop is, why it's important that you get there soon and what tasks now need to be rolled forward to the next day. If you were pinning your hopes on catching something to eat and your snares are empty, then work out exactly why you didn't succeed, adjust your set up and get started foraging for edible plants or even insects. Even just writing out the problem, making lists, putting things in order, will help. Nothing is worse than aimless drifting. I carry a notebook with me all the time, because I want to record what happens in case it's useful, but also because the act of writing or recording is always a positive way to finish each day and prepare for the next.

The key to motivating yourself as you seek to execute your plan – in any context – is to have an ultimate motivational goal that you can reach by a planned route of achievable, smaller ones. So how do we do this? If you stop trying in survival, the path you're on leads ultimately to death. But how do we go about forging our motivation, our belief that we can prevail, our hope? Laboratory experiments have proved that suffering on its own does not lead to a feeling of hopelessness. Importantly, hopelessness comes from suffering that we think we can't control.[20] Therefore, if we can maintain control of our suffering via our efforts, we can maintain our hope. This is key.

If we're able to break down the largest things we need to do into small achievable units, then we can proceed through them, and if we can proceed through them, we feel under control. If you're unhappy at work and want to change career, it might feel too huge a thing to even get started with. But if you break this into small, achievable units: signing up with three recruitment agencies in the next two weeks, writing a new CV in the next month, applying for two jobs in the next month, then the largest goal becomes a logical extension of each of the previous ones. When you move forwards through your tasks, you create hope, and as long as you can do that, you'll give yourself the best chance of keeping inside the lifeboat.

So we've seen how bad things happen when hope is lost. I want to balance out Denny's story with one of my favourite survival stories that illustrates how the opposite can be true.

Frank, Phil and George

In May 1942, three young airmen from the Royal Australian Air Force were sent to medically evacuate – 'medevac' – a soldier from a remote outpost. To do this, the three – Frank Smallhorn, the pilot; Phil Bronk, the medic; and George

Booth, the radio operator – had to fly across one of the most sparse and inhospitable regions of Northern Australia, Arnhem Land, in their small Tugan Gannet plane.

Arnhem Land is a vast zone – 97,000 square kilometres – bigger than the US State of South Carolina, and much hotter, swampier and stickier. It has plenty of trees but, because of the low ground, fresh water can be very hard to find and the many tidal rivers that web the area they had to cross were teeming with huge, man-eating saltwater croco- diles. On the plus side, the survival challenges of Arnhem Land meant that there was an established search and rescue plan for downed aviators. The crew knew that if there was a problem, other aircraft would be launched and a search would go on for a week along their flightpath. They'd had no survival training but they were young, fit and inventive.

Their problems began mid-flight when they were repeat- edly unable to raise other bases on the Gannet's radio, which had happened previously to aircraft transiting through the area. Although communication had failed for others, not being able to use their radio made George feel guilty; he was relatively new on the team and didn't want to let the side down. So, they couldn't talk to anyone, but it also meant that they were unable to get accurate position fixes by radio as they cloud-dodged their way across a broad, featureless landscape. The more they flew on, the more lost they became. In navigation, especially when you're travel- ling fast, small errors followed by more small errors quickly compound into big ones: they were getting loster and losterer. George started to tap out SOS messages.* No one answered.

Eventually, while they still had fuel, Frank decided to put the Gannet aircraft down to see if they could fix the radio and their position. There were no wide beaches in view – the coast wasn't even visible – but the terrain below looked fairly familiar; firm, grassy and flat enough to land on. Unfortunately, on touchdown it turned out to be soft and swampy; suddenly incredibly dangerous. As they decelerated too rapidly, the wings stopped providing lift, which then put the full weight of the aircraft onto the main wheels, causing them to dig into the smelly dark mud. And when the wheels dug in further, it caused the aircraft to flip violently forwards onto its nose at around 40 mph. Inside the aircraft, Frank the pilot lurched forwards in his seat harness and bashed his head on the controls. Both Phil and George were catapulted towards the tail end of the fuselage as it swung in a wide arc over the bogged-in wheels and smashed down to a halt, upside down.

As the detritus inside the airframe settled – that combination of muck and dust common to the interior of all general aviation – the crew came to their senses. Frank

---

* SOS in Morse code – three dots, three dashes, three dots ($\cdots$ $---$ $\cdots$) – is sometimes interpreted as 'Save Our Souls', but is actually just an unmistakeable nine-character 'set' in Morse. It was chosen as an internationally recognizable distress call and was first tapped out in anger by the RMS *Slavonia* as she sank in 1909, not – as is often claimed down at the pub – by the *Titanic*, which sank in 1912.

had cut his head but quickly made it outside, and then beckoned the others out too; he could smell petrol and there was a real risk of fire. They scrambled out and stood clear but luckily the hot engines were now immersed in the wet mud. As the aircraft lay inverted, with its muddy wheels pointing skywards, they watched but no fire erupted. Luckily too, no one had any serious injuries, although many big bruises would appear later.

What to do next? Well, they knew that the RAAF regulations said they were to stay put for seven days while a search got underway, so how could they help their would-be rescuers find them? George's top priority became getting the battery out of the aircraft – it was upside down and dripping out irreplaceable acid – and the battery was their only way of powering the radio. They attacked its compartment with their fire axe and had it out and right-way-up in minutes. George then started to remove, much more delicately, the whole radio set.

While he did that, Frank and Phil gathered the aircraft's signal lamp and flare pistol, then put out visual markers on the ground to attract the attention of search aircraft. They built a bonfire that they prepared for quick lighting with aviation fuel, and Frank added the aircraft's tyres, so that when lit the fire would produce black rubbery smoke that would stand out against the landscape. Lastly, almost as an afterthought, Phil opened out his parachute; it would make a big contrasting white circle on the tan ground when viewed from a search plane, a perfect polka dot among the otherwise jumbled geometry of the landscape. Unlike the other location aids they'd gathered and made, the parachute didn't need to be turned on or ignited – it could constantly draw attention to their position from above and required no effort from them. So they added a version that could be seen by any ground search party or friendly Aboriginal locals too; they attached a medical bedsheet to a tall sapling that would flap about in the breeze.

As for somewhere to spend the night, their medevac aircraft had two fixed stretchers; even though they were upside down they made good beds, and Frank the pilot slept on the floor – previously the Gannet's ceiling. Not claiming a comfortable bed, even though he was highest ranking as sergeant, was a gesture that was appreciated by the others and I think probably stemmed from a feeling of guilt that he'd got them into this mess with a botched landing.

Back together at the side of the aircraft, what they tackled next was a complete inventory of all useful stuff. This included Phil's medical kit, with which he dressed Frank's head wound, and the aircraft emergency pack containing twelve tins of baked beans and bully beef, two packets of currant biscuits, four small tins of concentrated chocolate and plenty of tea. They decided to use their food sparingly, even though they were confident that a search and rescue effort would soon find them. They opted for two meals a day, each made up of a tin of bully beef or beans divided three ways, one biscuit, one piece of chocolate and one 'cuppa'.

What was left of the daylight was spent by George trying

to make contact with the outside world using the radio. He'd rigged the antenna wire from the tailwheel to one of the main wheel struts and he'd carefully insulated it with medical tape where it touched. He now listened for the strongest signals – he could receive transmissions fine – and sent back SOS after SOS on those frequencies. His radio kit was displaying 'low' on transmission strength though, and they heard no responses to his calls for help. They didn't see or hear any search aircraft on the first day.

Let's just take a moment to notice how, at this early stage, they were constantly giving themselves things to do: inventory, tasks, problems to be solved. They were moving themselves out of threat mode and into problem-solving mode.

Throughout this time they'd been plagued by flies. As dusk settled in, the flies went off shift, only to be replaced by 'billions' of mosquitoes.[21] They tried to improvise a repellent from the Dettol and meths in the medical kit without much success. It was absolute torment, and the only escape was to get into bed and cover up completely with a blanket. That made them sweat heavily but it was the lesser of two evils; swaddling themselves in sweaty blankets beat being eaten alive, hands down.

The next day dawned and quickly grew stiflingly hot. They spent their waiting time by working the radio, and Phil made sure they were thoroughly familiar with his medical equipment and supplies, which included brandy and morphine. Frank applied himself to working out their exact location from his maps and improvising useful items from salvaged equipment. He was constantly busy. They even managed to create a radio direction-finding aerial from an old coat hanger, which enabled them to confirm their estimated position on the map. They had strayed a long way north of their intended flight path. Later, a little rain came and added to their drinking-water supplies. Frank and Phil made a trip to check out the nearest river. They were gone for three hours and when they got back Phil looked ill; he thought the effort had triggered a return of his dengue fever. Worse still, the river was a mere stream with wide, muddy banks that made any crossing impossible. The sun set, the flies and mosquitoes did their shift change, and there was still no sign of a rescue aircraft.

The next day followed a similar pattern, with the added discovery of some cigarettes and a camera in the Gannet's locked rear stowage compartment. They took four photos of themselves and the upturned aircraft at the crash site. They also found some spare clothes belonging to another pilot to add to their meagre assortment of shorts, short-sleeved shirts and pith helmets. No sign of any searching aircraft.

As the days wore on the radio's batteries gradually ran out, at first meaning no transmissions could be made from their site, but still allowing George to listen to Morse and voice calls from other stations. In the transmissions he eavesdropped no one mentioned them or their plight, and he hunted the airwaves for music to ease their boredom, but found none. Then the battery became too weak even to just listen to Morse code – their radio was dead. No aircraft were seen or heard.

On day five, George accompanied Frank on another recce of the river, only to return exhausted, disappointed and covered up to his waist in mud, but with a growing admiration for Frank's boundless energy and optimism. In that day's rain shower they cleaned off the stinking mud with medical soap. No search planes came near.

In George's diary for day six, he contemplates using the morphine to overdose if they eventually ran out of food and water. They rested and scanned the horizons for aircraft, straining their ears for any sounds of engines. None came.

By day eight, they were 'utterly wretched'. No planes, no possibility of escape, and now the seven-day search window was definitely closed. They believed that only a miracle could save them; that they would die there. It's clear that the fundamental human responses were the same as those of the men in the jolly boat and over pretty much exactly the same time frame. So what happened differently from then on?

The seven-day search window in Arnhem Land had closed. Frank, a religious man, told George that he would stop saying Hail Marys and start praying to St Christopher. 'Who's he?' asked George, with more lethargy than interest. Before they became lost forever, and beyond even St

Christopher's help, on the ninth day Frank took George for another look at the river; the crew had no doubt that their survival and rescue was in their own hands now. Their survival depended upon getting out. When they got to its banks, the stream had transformed into a broad, flowing river; the Arnhem Land tides had brought them their miracle. What had been an obstacle was now a route out, and they could form a travel plan.

Here I want to recognize a fundamental difference between this situation and that of the SS *Anglo Saxon* survivors. The Australian aircrew were able to look for an exit; and by looking they caught a break. If the jolly boat had made land after eight or nine days, if they'd had a chance to take on provisions, then things could have been very different. But it's also important to recognize that you don't catch the break if you've already given up. If they hadn't summoned up the energy to go to the river that last time, they'd never have realized things had changed. Because they had harnessed the power of hope by finding problems they could solve, they had the energy to keep going until the one they couldn't was solved for them.

You miss 100 per cent of the shots you don't take.

Let's keep looking at how Frank, George and Phil were able to continually sustain hope throughout their ordeal, which was really only just beginning.

According to their map, which was pretty sparse on detail, the nearest known settlement was around 150 miles away – a missionary outpost on the coast. If they could make a raft they could float to the sea with the tides, then follow the coast until they reached the outpost. Plus there was always the chance of encountering friendly locals en route, the Aboriginal people who had lived and prospered in this landscape for millennia.

They set-to building a raft, using the aircraft's four fuel tanks for flotation, their openings sealed with black tar-like gunk from the dead batteries, and then lashed together a two by three metre frame of saplings with cord from the parachute. They added a sapling as a mast, enabling them to rig some shade with parachute material. This could also help them later if they needed to sail, but for now they cut a long pole to propel them along and steer with. The build took a day and a half of endless cutting, trimming, dragging and knot tying in the sucking mud and energy-sapping heat at the bank. When they'd finished, Phil stung their raw hands clean with iodine from the medical kit to prevent infection.

The whole endeavour tested the determination of Phil and George, who were motivated in part by attempting to keep up with Frank, who although just out of his teens, was leading by dogged good example. He, in turn, was driven by a feeling of guilt – that as the pilot he had flown them all into this predicament – and he was determined to lead them out of it. Phil and George had tried to convince him otherwise, but Frank's feeling of intense responsibility still persisted.

It's interesting how the same guilt that Denny felt is used here as a positive force, because it was channelled into practical steps.

Once the raft was finished, they chose what to take and what to leave to rot in the swamp. With them came a handgun, the medical kit, a blanket each, a parachute, some waterproofed matches, the signal lamp, the flare pistol, their water tanks, two billy cans, the little remaining food, the map and compass, and an assortment of tools that they considered useful for survival.

Having studied the ebb and flow of the river during all the work at the riverbank, they estimated that seven in the morning would be the best time to launch. They toasted the upcoming trip the next day with cold tea and a splash of brandy and, most importantly, renewed hope and humour. At the allotted morning hour they were relieved to see the raft bob like a cork as it was gently edged into the coffee-coloured flow. She was named *Santa Maria* by Frank. Their journey out of the swamp had begun.

With all the stores carefully tied to the raft, Frank and Phil sat at the front and George perched on the uncomfortably narrow saplings across the *Santa Maria*'s stern. She moved with the tidal flow at a brisk walking pace; certainly faster than they could have walked after twelve days of very limited food intake. A gentle breeze from the north-east was helping to push them on their way; the only real effort being made was by George at the back as he used the barge pole to prevent them running aground on the river's many meandering bends.

At around eleven, the mudbanks were beginning to be revealed on the inside of the bends and George was having to use the pole more frequently to stay in the main channel of the river. As he pushed them clear once more he noticed an old muddy tree trunk half stuck in the flat bank. Suddenly it developed legs and rushed at the raft, and George recoiled from the charging saltwater crocodile as Phil and Frank looked on helplessly. Saltwater crocodiles, 'salties', can grow to huge proportions – over twenty-five feet long – and regularly attack boats and people. Luckily for the crew, this five-metre long specimen had made a direct track to the water when it was disturbed by the pole, but George was badly shaken. He sat on his haunches, moaning over and over, and would have recurring nightmares about it afterwards.

George liked to chat and he had been a schoolteacher before the war, so in order to ease him out of shock the others asked him what he knew about salties. As he was telling them, Frank quietly and slowly drew his revolver and pointed it towards the back of the raft. George looked round, and there, two metres from him, the croc was gliding through the water behind them, stalking the raft. Frank handed George the gun. 'It's cocked. If he opens his mouth, put a slug down his throat. It might just upset him.' Their anti-'nearest crocodile' plan was formed. As an aside, I think this is a wonderful way of remembering that though you should always pay attention to the thing that's going to harm you soonest, you should stick to your long-term goal.

The saltie didn't attack, nor did any of the other forty or fifty that they saw as their raft made its way slowly towards the sea. At one point, five were trailing them at once; it's hard to imagine how vulnerable that would make you feel, floating four inches above muddy crocodile-infested water on a raft held together by bits of string.

As the light faded and the river's seaward flow stopped, they tied off to a tree to await the next tide. Clouds of mosquitoes soon replaced crocodiles as the main biters. They made themselves as comfortable as they could with folded blankets and saplings for seats. Hours later, at around midnight, the raft slowly turned on its tether line and they felt the river once more begin to pull in the right direction. They cast off and continued towards the coast in total darkness.

After a few more hours of slow progress, their motion stopped again, but there were no mosquitoes and no coughing crocodiles to be heard in the dark. Their twelfth day in Arnhem Land dawned in dense fog; they'd drifted out to sea. As the sun rose higher, the fog burned off and visibility improved. Frank began to match distant landmarks to his map. There was another feature that appeared as they looked down into the deep, clear water beneath them. Sharks. A new entourage now accompanied them.

The land gradually warmed up and the day's breeze developed, so they re-rigged the parachute material from shade to sail and with it made better progress towards the island mission station, their ultimate goal. As more land features revealed themselves, Frank pinpointed their position on the map. Combining that with their direction and rate of movement, he worked out that the next hazard they faced was a peninsula – 'Flinders' – that blocked their progress. They knew that making landfall in a rickety raft floating on fragile fuel tanks would be dangerous for their survival prospects. Another plan was required.

As a surf-club rower before war broke out, George came up with a drill for them all to follow once they entered the surf zone of the shore. Being able to decide on this, and brief the others on what to do, boosted his sense of usefulness and his morale.

This is another key thing to keep in mind. Human beings like to feel that they are impacting a situation personally. We get both the satisfaction of problem solving, plus the pleasure of knowing that we are gaining recognition for what we've done within our social group. If we can harness the power of both, we have a powerful motivator to keep going.

The others did as George instructed – rechecking the lashings for all their equipment and finally tying paracord lifelines between themselves and the raft. When the time came they did as George directed, lowering the sail and then getting off the raft to prevent it toppling, while holding on tight and trying to stay away from its front as the whole party were hurled onshore. They'd been on the *Santa Maria* for thirty-six hours when they finally felt terra firma. They were exhausted and cold, but they dragged their raft above the high tide line, lit a fire and fell asleep.

After the last of the rations were had for breakfast, they spent the next day resting and eating shellfish to regain their strength. Oysters, crabs and periwinkles were plentiful and it took no effort to gather lots. Frank shared his knowledge by showing the other two how to use the medical kit's surgical safety pins to tease out the slug-like periwinkle from its shell once cooked. More importantly, their water supplies had dwindled to almost a quarter of what they'd started with. They limited their intake from this point to five mouthfuls a day and established a strict practice of resting in the shade during the midday heat to prevent sweating.

Their next goal en route to the mission station was to relaunch the raft out and away from the dangerous shore. By now they'd tuned in to their environment, and realized that the onshore breezes in daylight would make that impossible. Their best launch window was going to be around midnight, when there would be no wind working against them and the ebbing tide would help to drag them out.

Starting at around one in the morning, they tried four times to get the formation of weakened bodies, saplings, paracord and fuel tanks past the surf by pushing and kicking, but they just couldn't manage it. They needed to re-work the plan and their inspiration came when Frank bemoaned Phil and George's efforts: '. . . you're a couple of no-hopers. You couldn't paddle your way out of a bathtub!' Ding – a lightbulb clicked on. They headed back up the beach.

That day, their fourteenth in Arnhem Land, was spent cutting up one of their billy cans with medical scissors, and tying the resulting pieces by paracord to the end of two saplings. Two forked sticks were cut and lashed to the raft as oarlocks for the *Santa Maria*'s brand-new paddles. That night at 1 a.m., they put the new rig to the test. It worked, and they were out to sea past the breakers once more; heading for their ultimate goal round the point of the peninsula. They had now established a way of landing and launching their craft, and the routine of resting in the shade during the midday heat helped conserve precious fluids. None of this was easy, sometimes making landfall on sharp coral was downright dangerous, but they knew they could keep repeating the sequence while they had water to drink. I've seen time and time again that a group's ability to carry out a task is more linked to gaining a feeling of control over it than to its intrinsic difficulty.

In this way they progressed, beach by beach, day by day, further up the coast towards salvation. They faced many problems, but used the same ingenuity and teamwork that had served them so well this far. One of the most critical points they would reach was when their fresh water supply ran out. You need lots of water to digest their protein-rich diet of seafood, not to mention to support their normal metabolism in the tropical heat, where even with enforced rest at midday they would be losing plenty of water just by sweating.

Just as their supply was running out, Phil used quiet observation to locate some more. He watched the birds. While sitting on the shore one day he noticed that there were more small birds than normal, that they were finches, so not seabirds, and that they were coming and going from a spot behind the beach in the trees. As he walked into the treeline to investigate, he also spotted that as the ground sloped down to where the birds were heading it got subtly greener in colour. It led him to a small pool of pure spring water, a life-saving needle in Arnhem Land's haystack. They could fight on.

On the twentieth day after the crash they finally made it to Elcho Island, marked on their map as having the Methodist mission, but the problem was that the island was thirty miles long and the map didn't say whereabouts the mission was. So now a new plan was needed; if they put the raft to sea they would be blown clear of the island's shore on the leeward side and be unable to make it back. Having tried towing and pushing the raft in the shallows they knew it was too energy-sapping. Their only option was to walk, but what to take with them?

Through their recent experiences they knew what was vital, so the decision of what to take was easy – but the act of leaving sentimental possessions was still hard. They took a few items of medical kit, some cutting tools, matches, and their water cans, which they carried with paracord across their shoulders, padded with a blanket that would keep them warm at night. And so the next phase of their epic ordeal began, walking anticlockwise around a thirty-mile-long tropical island, carrying heavy but essential loads while looking for any sign of friendly local people.

They walked for days and got progressively weaker, covering less distance each morning and afternoon. Even getting up after their shady midday rest required help from one of the others. Phil was fading fastest, and Frank, who had a little more energy, ended up carrying Phil's load as well as his own, all the while coaxing and encouraging the other two onwards. The first sign of life they saw came on the third day of trudging, when they discovered a long-since abandoned Aboriginal camp, unfortunately without any fresh water source. By the fourth day they neared the island's northern end, and it was then that they had their Robinson Crusoe moment; footprints in the sand. It was the first sign of another living human in over three weeks – their spirits soared and they camped that night by the footprints, but no one came.

The next morning, their fifth on Elcho and twenty-five days since the crash, they set off northwards for the tip of the island. Pretty soon they saw more footprints of different sizes, and those of a dog. Then they saw a path into the trees on their left. They followed it and every few feet there was a freshly cut sapling laying across the path. They put down their loads and ventured further, not knowing what to expect. In a cleared area ahead lay a felled tree, which had been turned into a dugout canoe. To one side of the clearing they saw, covered with pieces of bark for shade, some bags made from paperbark. George picked one up, but Frank wasn't sure it was a good idea. 'Just one won't hurt, Frank!' he said. 'This one is bulging with food. I bet this is a coconut!' George undid the bag and pulled out a human skull.

After a very brief discussion on the proximity of known cannibals, they replaced everything they'd found, which also included items from the island's Christian ministry, and moved off to make a fireless camp. They discussed the mission and the contact that the canoe builders must've had, and they knew that locals in this region were encouraged to help Allied airmen. So they put the skull's presence down to some other tradition and focused on the positive aspects of getting outside help. Context was everything in maintaining a sense of optimism.

Next morning, a beautiful Arnhem Land day broke to the crackle of their breakfast fire and by-now customary periwinkle soup. As the exhausted men stared at the horizon, a tall dark figure appeared in the distance, way down the beach. He strode purposefully towards them, carrying not

weapons but a small child on his shoulders, a truly internationally recognizable non-threatening posture. His name
was Matui, but he introduced himself in pidgin English by
his missionary name, Paddy. He was the main man on Elcho
Island and, smiling, said he would help Frank, George and
Phil to get home. It would take another week, and several
dangerous sea crossings by dugout canoe, but they had
finally found their salvation in the wilderness, after twenty-
six days of constant unaided enterprise and endeavour.

You can be a drifter or a doer

There are many parallels when we put the stories of Frank,
George and Phil and the crew of the SS *Anglo Saxon* next to
each other. But we see the difference that small achievable
tasks, agency and hope makes. By agency I mean the ability
to change your own circumstances. In a small boat, drifting
in the sea, there is literally almost nothing you can do to
change your circumstances. Other than wait to sight land
or jump off the boat. But Frank, George and Phil were able
to break down their endeavour into smaller, achievable
units throughout. They were able to constantly find ways
to change their situation and therefore feel they were progressing. At every stage, they were able to find the next
thing they could do, and by doing it they maintained their
hope.

Realistic optimism

Admiral James Stockdale was a US Navy pilot, held for over seven years by the North Vietnamese – he was their most senior-ranked prisoner. He was also a philosopher, a Stanford graduate student of Stoicism, which is often used as common shorthand for the endurance of pain or hardship without complaint, but in fact is also a much broader and very useful philosophy for any situation. During his captivity he was tortured many times and held in solitary confinement for four years – in leg irons for two years – with a lightbulb continually on. Hard to even begin to imagine.

He observed the behaviour of many other US POWs during his almost eight years in captivity and he noticed a pattern. Counter-intuitively, the prisoners who didn't survive were optimists, but crucially their optimism was blind; theirs was hope in denial of reality. By telling themselves that they would be out by Christmas, with no evidence at all to suggest that, they were psychologically crushed when release didn't come on time. This unexpected situation of optimism causing despondency was christened the 'Stockdale Paradox' by author Jim Collins, after he interviewed the admiral philosopher years later.

Lasting hope can only be borne out of realistic optimism; created by analysing the detail of the problem and working out what is possible for us to control. After his ordeal, James Stockdale put into writing his own thoughts about how he had managed to survive those years, what was actually required to prevail in those darkest of realities. As he ejected from his plane he carried with him:

> . . . the understanding that a Stoic always kept separate files in his mind for those things that are 'up to him' and those things that are 'not up to him'. Another way of saying it is those things which are 'within his power' and those things which are 'beyond his power'. Up to me, within my power, within my will, are my opinions, my aims, my aversions . . . my attitude about what is going on.

His paper was entitled 'Master of My Fate',[22] and it provides an inspiring resource for not only dealing with extreme situations like his, but everyday life too.

So how do we do this?

With our own personalized PLAN, as per Chapter 2, we should have established our priorities. Now we can begin the series of required small steps towards survival by matching our abilities to achievable goals. Then the work to be done is reaching those goals, one by one, through effort, improving your situation as you go. Controlling the situation, allowing the conditions for realistic optimism to thrive.

A good way to reach smaller, stepping-stone goals in your everyday is to set yourself a small time limit to carry them out. If you can't change the size of the task, you can at least break it into smaller units of time. This is especially effective when it's a job that you don't enjoy; when there's no actual satisfaction in the task itself. The next time you're in that situation, try a twenty-five minute activity spurt, followed by a five-minute break – part respite, part reward for your efforts – before you start again. This short time frame will also help to maintain your effort levels and mental focus on the task at hand. Quite often, having this short, sharp approach sees the whole task completed much sooner than you estimated, so you can have a longer break as a pat on the back from yourself at the end. When I'm working on anything that's more physical than mental, I find that doubling this up to a fifty-minute work window followed by a ten-minute rest is good; that's about long enough for a brew. Very often we approach our days as two three-and-a-half-hour chunks either side of lunch, each with multiple tasks, all interspersed with responding to email. Once it becomes seven fifty-minute chunks, or fourteen twenty-five-minute chunks, or a combination of the two, we can match this up to our task list much more easily. As we saw in Chapter 2, the trick is to move this out of our brain's threat-response area and into a more rational space.

Setting a series of small achievable goals, 'little victories', that link up in a continuous chain towards the ultimate goal is the way to tackle any difficult situation.

The force that powers your motivation to work is hope. You maintain it when you see that your efforts are having an effect on your situation; you have some control. Even if the effect of your effort is just a small change, we recognize that lots of smaller changes add up to a big change. This is how to cultivate realistic optimism, and therefore perseverance. It is what helps us to feel like we're making our way slowly and steadily across terrain, whatever obstacles it throws at us, rather than lying passively in a lifeboat. If you prioritize, plan and work to change your situation, you'll nurture hope, sustaining your efforts and giving yourself the best possible chance of success.

Summary

→ Survival Triangle: the key to persevering through any tough patch is maintaining HOPE. A feeling of hopelessness is avoidable if you feel like you have some control over events. Control is gained when your planned efforts change your circumstances, however subtly. So form a plan of smaller goals, start working towards the nearest one, and keep pressing on as you make small changes that lead to big results.

→ Set short time limits, perhaps twenty-five minutes, for effort on unpleasant tasks. Stop at the allotted time and take a short break, say five minutes, away from the source of the nausea. Repeat until done. It'll be smashed through a lot quicker this way than if you tried to just slog it out in one long stint.

→ Everyone has something they can add. It may be that it's a skill from a previous job, or knowledge gained pursuing a hobby, but success in anything is easiest when it's a team effort where tasks are shared.

→ Realistic optimism: we can only create this important state of mind by analysing the detail of any problem and working out what is out of our hands, and what is possible for us to control. Focus on the things you can control, and don't waste your vital energy on the rest.

→ It's always better to have tried and failed than to have never tried at all. You will miss 100 per cent of the shots you don't take.

So now we know that hope is absolutely key to survival, as is breaking things into small, achievable chunks. But so far, we've mainly concentrated on what we can do inside our own heads. What about other people?

Chapter 5

THE IMPORTANCE OF OTHER PEOPLE

In 1719, Daniel Defoe's *Robinson Crusoe*, one of the most famous explorations of survival in all of literature, was published. Though it was fiction, the first edition listed the author as Robinson Crusoe, and many people believed it to be a memoir. It has gone on to be one of the most widely published novels in history and adapted countless times. But what you may not know is that it was based on a real castaway called Alexander Selkirk.

In September 1704, Selkirk was marooned – deliberately put ashore alone – on a deserted island called Más a Tierra in the South Pacific, hundreds of miles off the coast of what is now Chile.* He was abandoned there by his captain after complaining about the dangerous state of his vessel, saying he would rather stay on the island than remain on such a dangerous ship. Though he regretted his decision and asked

---

* It was renamed 'Robinson Crusoe Island' by Chile in 1966.

to be allowed back, only to be refused by the captain, he was ultimately proved right; the ship later sank, and few survived.

Selkirk was left with some useful items – a pistol and ammunition, an axe, a knife, a cooking pot, navigation instruments, a bible, some rum and tobacco. The island had lots of water and food, and a mild climate.

It didn't take him long to establish a routine where he went beyond mere survival to physically thriving on the island's ample resources. When his clothes wore out he made leather ones from the skins of the many feral goats that inhabited the island and formed a large part of his diet. He kept a calendar, carved into a tree, near his self-built stone-hearthed hut, using the moon's phases to chart his four-year tenure.

The challenge of hacking it alone in any remote spot goes deeper than just physical endurance. Selkirk was one of the first survivors whose experiences allow us to imagine the greatest problem of this classic scenario; isolation. The lack of the company of other humans was the main challenge that Selkirk faced daily. His routine revolved around keeping a lookout for ships; it became his obsession. He had a private island kingdom of his own – he was the original monarch of all he surveyed – but once he'd attended to his basic functional needs he longed to leave, to rejoin the imperfect society aboard a ship.

His dilemma was that not just any ship that he sighted

would do; if he were picked up by the Spanish he'd be imprisoned into forced labour in some South American silver mine. He needed to spot an English ship – he wasn't lonely enough to swap isolation for incarceration. Years passed before he eventually saw a ship approaching . . . but it was a Spanish vessel visiting his island to resupply. Selkirk hid up a tree while they ransacked his possessions and burned his hut down. Back to square one.

His hut, and the second one he built to replace the one burned by the Spanish, was a real draw to the island's massive rat population. He had a separate area for storing and cooking food, but the rats still ran amok in his living quarters, especially at night while he tried to sleep. When ships visit islands, rats go ashore. They're a part of the desert island experience that doesn't normally get top billing in the fantasy version, and once they escape ashore from a ship, rats are prodigious at making more rats.

So, to stop the rats from crawling over him and nibbling his skin while he tried to sleep, Selkirk domesticated feral cats, also on the island after their forebears escaped from visiting ships. The cats also kept him company, and he kept their kittens as pets as well as for pest control. Looking after them was a job which he drew satisfaction from, and as we've seen, that kind of positive feedback loop really helps.

Selkirk thought more and more about the church as time passed – his only reading material was a bible – and he knew that there was no one there to give him a decent burial if he stopped surviving. So, he thought, if he fell ill and succumbed – died – what would happen next? It didn't take long for him to realize that he *had to stay alive*, if only to avoid the indignity of being eaten by his many cats.

When rescue did finally appear after four years and four months, in January 1709, what they found was a young man in phenomenally good physical health but with wild, haggard eyes and a desperation to be among other humans. As the sailors closed in on him, all that Selkirk could utter was a hoarse 'marooned', then he wept. Whether or not we consider ourselves to be introverted, extraverted or even ambiverted, as humans we are all social creatures. There are exceptions to every rule and the ones to this rule are called sociopaths. So far, we've tended to focus on survival as it relates to self-reliance and small groups under pressure, but as with Chapter 4, where we were looking at how we can hook into our deepest level of motivation, we need to understand just how important being with others is to us and how our understanding of this can help us in our everyday lives.

Not just surviving

When Abraham Maslow wrote his seminal paper on the hierarchy of human needs, 'A Theory of Human Motivation', back in 1943, he listed our needs in order of importance as: Physiological; Safety; Love (now also called *Belonging*); Esteem; and finally, at the top of his pyramid, Self-Actualization (which means being able to find meaning in life).[23] In other words, once we're out of physical danger the next thing we want is to be with our tribe, our social group; to belong. So far, we've covered the pure Physiological in some detail and touched on Belonging, but it's time now for us to think about Belonging, Esteem and Self-Actualization and how they interrelate and impact on our ability to execute our personalized PLAN.

The negative effects of isolation have been known for years, and the United Nations now considers prolonged solitary confinement to be 'cruel, inhuman or degrading treatment' that may amount to torture. In extreme cases, isolation can lead to complete psychological collapse. We need to be in contact with other people. Psychologists have shown that even a small amount of social interaction can make a massive difference to our sense of happiness and motivation.[24] As we've discussed, an implicit goal of survival is to return to society, to those we love. Some people unwittingly engage in a degree of self-imposed isolation; one of the top regrets of those at the end of their lives is that they spent too much time working and not enough quality time with their loved ones, family and friends.

How can we avoid replicating this kind of isolation at home? If the research I referred to above – which was carried out by palliative care nurses trying to establish the top regrets of those at the end of their lives – teaches us one thing, it's that we should prioritize meaningful time with our loved ones over more time at work.

We must never forget the comfort and motivation that finding pleasure in having the right people around us can bring. But we also have to admit that that isn't always the case. All too often, the things that cause us to feel defensive, to start making assumptions and to make bad choices, involve other people. Perhaps it's a colleague at work who seems to constantly undermine us, or a boss that doesn't seem to notice the effort we put in. However much we might be focused on self-reliance, on taking care of our own business, other people can get in the way. I spend a lot of my time working with groups of people under pressure, and I want to take you through a few things that I've observed first hand.

Other people's intentions

By now you'll probably be able to guess what our brains do when we first meet someone. Yes, we tend to see them as a potential threat. Back in the day, when we lived in small, closely knit groups, competing for resources, this made a lot of sense. The people that spent too much time wondering if that stranger from the mountain tribe might actually be a really great guy underneath it all more often than not wouldn't last long. But that's not quite the same in the average work environment. However, we still apply that model, leaping to the defensive as our default position. This response is heightened if we perceive that person to be different to us.

Other people's behaviours

This defensive response is compounded by the fact that we're just not very good at working out why people behave the way they do. That person wincing at the coffee machine as you tell a story might be undermining you in front of your colleagues, or they might have a bad back. There have been repeated studies that prove that when we try and guess at other people's behaviour we ascribe it to their character, but when thinking about our own behaviour we ascribe it to context.[25] So if a stranger shakes their fist when someone cuts them up in traffic, it's because they're an angry person who can't control themselves. When we do it, the other driver was being really dangerous, we wanted to signal that to them, it's been a long day, we have a headache, etc. If someone else is late to a meeting, it's because they're disrespectful; if we're late, it's because of circumstances beyond our control.

When we're out training, we have to battle against this constantly. If there's someone not trying as hard as everyone else, or consistently doing less heavy lifting than every-one else, it's tempting to file them away as 'lazy' in your head or that they're a 'shirker'. But I've found it instructive to try and imagine their context: are they injured or recover-ing from illness? Are their socks twisted? I try and think about all the things that might factor into me not being at my best and always err on the side of giving them the ben-efit of the doubt. Next time someone behaves in a way that angers or frustrates you, try and think what might have hap-pened to make them act like that and try and focus on con-text, not character. Think about how often things that no one else knows about can impact how you behave – a head-ache, a family problem, an argument at home – and then give them the same benefit of the doubt you would hope others give you.

Common ground

I also see, at first hand, how groups of people bond under pressure. Very often there is a lot of competition between new instructors, to show who is best, toughest or most experienced, and this can lead to conflict. The first rule is that the quickest route to bonding seems to be finding something in common. And by that I mean something out-side of the fact 'you're trudging through this bog too'. I've lost track of the number of times people have struck up conversations about shared hobbies, or interests, bands or sports teams. This means that when the pressure is on they're far more likely to respond to each other as human beings first, rather than an obstacle that needs to be overcome. This can sometimes be awkward to introduce if you don't have that sort of relationship with colleagues, so start small. Use the barber's trick and ask someone on a Friday what they've got planned that weekend and let them know what you have planned too. People are far more likely to interact if they feel they've got something back from you in return. You might have experienced this with the office gossip, who will confide a secret they know about someone, in the hope that you'll reciprocate. It's almost impossible to feel like you don't owe them something. Use this for good, and rather than gossip, see what happens if you confide something personal to a normal team member. It doesn't have to be a deep secret, just something that reveals a bit more about what makes you tick.

Bringing other people with you

Very often in life, we need not only to understand what motivates someone to behave in a certain way, but also to try and bring them with us. We've seen countless examples of situations where people have to decide what to do next. And we also know from our own experiences that often going along with someone is as much down to how persuasive they are as the actual idea they're pitching. I've worked in high-pressure environments where we need to get across crucial information quickly and persuasively. So how do you help give your idea the best chance of being listened to? How do you bring other people with you, make your ideas more 'sticky' in their brains?

A useful thing to know about how we make information or ideas last longer in our memory banks, is that we remember things better when they are explained in the form of a story. We follow the facts and key events best when they are laid out like Hansel and Gretel's breadcrumbs; in a context that we can mentally visualize. A great friend of mine is fond of saying, 'a good story should have a beginning, a middle and an end'. I agree completely, and it should also have characters, a challenge, a choice and a resolution. If all of these story ingredients can be combined to convey useful information, then it is more likely to be remembered as useful knowledge by the listener. This type of survival training uses what is known as a 'semantic memory', something you remember colloquially, not from personal experience, and understand without necessarily knowing the full science involved. It's through stories that we can best embed the knowledge that your body needs water before food, and make that knowledge stick.

We like to take mental shortcuts, and colourful stories fit the bill. Our ancestors knew this too; long before writing was developed, cultures passed on their survival knowledge via oral histories. In some cultures these even evolved into songs that the whole group would learn by singing together around the fire.

My advice is to tell stories that are emotive, rather than just factual. Remember when we were learning about the points in our evolution where different parts of the brain developed, right at the beginning of the book? The parts of our brain that relate to basic emotions are far older than the parts that relate to abstract thought or logic. If I'm trying to make a lesson stick about why you should make sure your boots fit more loosely in the Arctic, I don't wheel out statistics or just explain the science, I tell them the story of my mate whose boots were too tight, meaning he nearly lost a toe to frostbite, then show them a photo of his frozen toe. Throughout this book, I've tried to lead with emotion and then pull back and uncover what we can learn.

What I've found is that in a battle between emotion and facts, emotion will almost always win. I've seen it play out again and again. A group are deciding between two options, and it's the idea that hooks the emotions that gets listened to, even if it's actually not as strong.

An easy way of evoking this response is to talk about a scenario in relation to people and how it will impact them. You can pitch someone that improving this element of your training will increase efficacy by 20 per cent, or you can quantify it in the number of people whose lives will be improved. Try out the difference between saying '25 per cent of people' and 'one in four people in this room'. It's a tiny change but it makes it much more likely to stick with someone. And try and include some element of surprise – it's this little hook that will get the story to stick with them.

Dress to impress

What we wear can have a huge effect, not only on how others see us, but also in how we perceive ourselves. This emerging field of psychology has been called enclothed cognition, and focuses on studying the effects of clothing on our brains. It's been found that when we wear clothing with the right cultural and role-specific cachet, we perform better. In lab tests experimenters used one particular garment – a simple white coat – and found that test subjects who'd been told it was a doctor's white coat performed better when they wore it. Those subjects who were not wearing one, or were told that exactly the same coat was a painter and decorator's jacket instead of a medical doctor's one, did not improve their test scores.[26] In short, the psychologists found that wearing the right clothes boosts your performance if they have the right symbolic meaning. Which explains, at least in part, why some new SERE instructors will often wash their field kit until it looks faded and well worn, thus making it more 'alley'.* This confirms

* Alley – *adj*. To look streetwise and tough, like an alley cat.

the old adage that it's not just what you wear, but how you wear it, that creates the complete effect. The right clothing, whether you're going up a mountain or down the high street, will affect your confidence. Knowing you're in the best clobber for the occasion will improve it; and your performance.

Perfect your swagger

One British evader knew about the psychology of wearing something with self-assurance, and then using that to hide in plain sight. It certainly wasn't just Lieutenant David James's outfit that allowed him to walk through Germany during the Second World War to eventual freedom, but how confidently he carried himself. Which is just as well, because he wore his full Royal Navy uniform while evading through enemy territory, and even spent a night as a guest in German military accommodation. It was the little details that helped him. He added, in small, gold stitching, the initials 'K.B.V.M.F.' to the shoulder of his tunic, standing for 'Kralov Bulgrski Voyenno Mrskoi Flot', or Royal Bulgarian Navy. Although Bulgaria was on the side of the Nazis, he knew it was unlikely that anyone would be familiar with their uniform. On top of that, the name he chose to put on his forged papers was Ivan Bagerov, pronounced 'I. Bugger-off'. It's the little things. But little details can make all the difference to your confidence, which explains why you'll perform much better at a normal job interview if you wear smarter clothes; the outfit matches the occasion, you feel less out of place and more relaxed, that makes you appear more confident, your chances of landing the dream job go up.

Training/learning best practice

The question that all good survival instructors ask, after 'has the kettle boiled?', is normally how to best pass their knowledge on to students. What is the best way of making the important stuff memorable, making the training better? We know that there are different styles of learning – some people much prefer audio to visual stimuli, some need to touch things more than others. You may already have preferences for how you learn new information, and these can vary from scenario to scenario. But there are a few techniques that work well for all of us, regardless of what we are trying to commit to memory.

What I've found over the years is that carrying a waterproof notebook is priceless. Being able to sketch down new observations whatever the weather, like leaf shapes on useful plants or shelter designs, allows me to revisit them later on in my hammock, thereby consolidating an experience as a 'learning event'. The latest research shows that we remember things far better if we draw them. In lab tests, subjects were able to recall more of a list of thirty words if they'd drawn them rather than written them out repeatedly.[27] It's thought that drawing something uses lots of different processes that are known to benefit memory, such as visualization and deeper-level elaborative thought. So the next time you want to remember something, doodle it. We're all so used to receiving information in long reams of text that breaking things up a little is always welcome.

When I have to give a survival talk, I combine a couple of these memory techniques. I will try to make the arc of the talk fit around a cool story, with one of the emotional hooks described earlier, like a life-threatening situation where we can try to imagine how we'd respond. Then, to cement the chain of details in my own head before I deliver the session, I draw it out, trying to use a single image to prompt each chunk of detail that I know. I find it far easier to recall sequences of images that I've doodled, and access the info in this way, than trying to note down hundreds of bullet points to memorize. This allows me to do my presentation without notes, which normally helps to free me up to move about more, adding more energy to my delivery.

Devices that connect us can often separate us

One of the benefits of spending a lot of time in environments where mobile phones either don't work, or it isn't advisable to reveal them to the elements, is that I see how they impact communication. I was recently teaching some brand-new military pilots how to survive in the woods and as we walked back to civilisation after the exercise, they spoke of how for the first few days they'd felt ghost vibrations from the pocket where their cell phone would normally sit. It was like they'd had their phones amputated and were feeling phantom messages and notifications arrive. What happened as time wore on though, was that they gradually rediscovered the pleasure of connecting with nature and focusing on actual conversations rather than texted ones. I think that making time for real-life interaction with other human beings is as essential as clean water and sleep. Another thing we see time and time again with people not used to the survival lifestyle is how much they relish talking. At first they're a bit awkward, not sure what to do with their hands if they're not pushing a touchscreen, but soon they remember the simple pleasure of talking, 'spinning dits' and finding out new things. When you next catch up with a good friend, keep that phone away for the entire time. There's nothing more likely to make someone check out of their engagement with you than the idea that you're only talking to them in the gaps between more important messages.

How to criticize

It's a fact of life that however you want to inspire and bring people with you, often you're going to have to give them feedback when they haven't done something right. It happens incredibly often in my day job of survival instructor training.

Here are my tips for these conversations. You have to start by praising something that they've done well; this comes hard to some of the military types I know. It has to be specific too, not just 'yeah, that was great, but . . .' People can see through that. You need to tell them what was good and then frame your feedback around how to improve on the good start they've already made. You have to imagine that your job is to trip the problem-solving pathways in their brain, and get them to feel a sense of realistic optimism. Our goal should be to help maximize these conditions in the people around us, as well as in our own lives. This skill can be especially important if you're suffering through extremis in a small group. Whenever people are low on energy and tensions are high, it's vital to frame criticism constructively rather than hitting others up with points that could sound like lists of personal failings. It's vital to maintain group morale and cohesion in these scenarios, so if you're in any doubt pause before you voice concerns to consider how they might be received.

How to praise

Though it's important to keep key principles in mind when we criticize other people, it's equally important that we are careful when and how we give praise. The wrong sort of praise can do harm. I've witnessed enough people grasp a new skill, which seemed impossible to them at first, to know how quickly focused effort can lead to success. What I've seen, time and time again as I train these new survival instructors is that, ultimately, the very best ones tend to be those who didn't 'get it' at first. When people take to something quickly there's a danger that they will believe that they have some kind of gift, that they're special. So whenever we're teaching, we've learned to only ever praise effort, never 'natural ability'. Praising 'talent' has been proven by psychologists to be very counterproductive. Praising effort instead of talent instils a 'growth mindset'.[28] An individual with a growth mindset will accept ownership of an issue. Once you accept that an issue is within your control you can then correct it with more effort; it can be *controlled*. People who believe they're naturally talented can become reliant on their 'natural ability', and assume that this will carry them through, even as tasks start to get harder and more complex. Of course, as the difficulty of the tasks increase it eventually exceeds whatever head start they had, and they fail to complete them. Then follows the internal monologue: 'Now what? How can I not meet this target when I'm so talented and I could do the other ones? Where do I go from here? If it's too much now, then I've got no chance of succeeding with the next one – why even bother trying? Best to stop now, while I'm still pretty awesome.'

It's not just nice to be nice, it's smart too

If we can focus on the things we can do to feel connected with people, it will not only make us and those around us happier, it's likely to make us perform better. I've witnessed group morale on an exercise unravel within hours as one world-class grumbler infected everyone else. In work it can be something as mundane as complaining about the weather or the quality of the coffee, but once that moaning ball starts rolling, it can undo huge amounts of effort everyone has been putting in to keep upbeat.

Studies by Harvard scientists have shown that emotions can be transmitted in the same way as infectious diseases[29] and others have shown that leaders are especially 'contagious'.[30] If you imagine that your personal morale is a small bag of optimism, with a maximum of one hundred shiny 'happy tokens' in it, here's how to work out what you have left after a trip to the survival shops. Each contented person you interact with puts another two tokens in your bag. Ace. Similarly, when you feel upbeat, it brings others around you up too, at no cost to you. Sadly, however, for every discontented person you have to interact with, four tokens disappear from your stash. It's a proven fact that 'moaners' are twice as damaging to your morale as light-hearted people are good for it.

We all know who the office drippers are, and how listening to them for too long makes us feel. Now imagine being trapped in a tight spot with them, when you're trying to keep your delicate candle flame of hope from going out in the survival gale. People's 'happy bucket' tends to be low to begin with in unexpected, harsh conditions, and it doesn't take long to empty if there's a drip. I was once lucky enough to chat to a couple who'd climbed Mount Everest together and also walked to both the South and North Poles, with just one another for company and support. One of their keys to harmony – written in permanent marker pen on the inside of their tent – was a rule: 'Only say nice things to each other.' I think that's a great general rule for normal life too. At its most extreme, negativity can convince someone to climb out of the lifeboat, and us with them.

Try actively minimizing the chances of your bad mood infecting others. If you know that you're a bit grumpy in the mornings, you can expect that to be even worse if you slept badly. Knowing that your mood can have a direct effect on others, why not take one for the team? Go and be grumpy at the coffee pot for five minutes, get it off your chest there instead of among the group you're working with. It's survival money in the bank.

That's one way of helping your team. If you find yourself in a low mood at any time and you want to help yourself as well, here's another neat little trick that will get your brain back on track, bringing you out of your funk. There's a large body of scientific research that has shown that the way we act or hold ourselves influences how we feel. There are nerve connections between muscle groups and our brains, and it demands almost zero effort to get them working for us. We know that when we feel happy we smile, but did you know that when you smile it makes you feel happy? Well it does. I'm not suggesting you start forcing yourself to maniacally grin though; there's a cheat. What the researchers discovered is that if you hold a pencil in your mouth crossways (ever seen a dog with a stick that looks sad?) it forces your facial muscles into the position they'd be in if you were smiling.[31] That's enough to make the feedback kick in and your brain get sent a message that says 'happy'. If you're at a desk and you need to use this cheat, people will just assume your pen's in your mouth while you type between notes; very industrious of you. We can work this to our advantage whenever we're feeling a bit down – if you need this boost in the great outdoors use a twig (yes, yes: clean and non-poisonous, etc., etc.). Caution: if you hold your pencil in your mouth by one end, rather than crossways, this puts your facial muscles into a more frowning, negative state, with corresponding results.

Sense of humour failure

Which segues nicely into recognizing one of the first signs that someone you know may be struggling to cope with something extreme in their world. The first sense that you lose in survival is your sense of humour. I see it all the time when I'm outdoors training survival instructors, or indoors coaching people on their presentation skills. When your brain is overloaded by complex problems you lose the capacity to crack jokes or laugh at yourself. You have a 'sense of humour failure'. Joke taking and giving is also one of the last things to come back online after a stressful event, which explains why 'banter' or 'piss-taking' is such a common feature of military groups; your sense of humour is a canary in the mine, warning you and others of high stress levels.

Through most of this chapter we've been talking about the importance of other people in relation to yourself or colleagues, but we also need to talk about leaders.

The disproportionate importance of good leaders

The story of the mutiny on HMS *Bounty* has been made famous from the standpoint of chief mutineer Fletcher Christian in many stage and screen versions. Whether you imagine Errol Flynn, Clark Gable, Marlon Brando, Mel Gibson – or even David Essex – as Fletcher, casting Cornishman Bligh and his small group adrift, we'll leave the story of why nineteen sailors came to be put into the twenty-three-foot-long launch for another day. When that mutiny happened in 1789, British sailors were the era's real-world equivalent of the crew from a modern-day science-fiction spacecraft. They ventured into regions with hostile climates and equally hostile inhabitants, speaking in unknown languages. They routinely travelled in small ships further than any preceding humans, and they had absolutely no prospect of rescue, nor means of getting home, if something went badly wrong. As a small cohort, Royal Navy sailors had seen more of our planet's remotest regions than anyone else who'd ever lived up to that time.

Bligh had already sailed around the globe; he was with Captain Cook's third voyage of discovery ten years earlier when the explorer was killed on Hawaii. During that period he made charts for Cook and the Admiralty – maps of Pacific islands in plain language – and although he was originally from a small village in Cornwall, he was about as well travelled a human as you could get. When Bligh and eighteen of his crew were cast adrift by the mutineers near Tonga in the Friendly Islands of the South Pacific, the nearest European outpost was over 4,000 miles away in Kupang, on the island of Timor. They survived because of Bligh's navigation – he managed to sail them the incredible distance using a compass, a sextant to take measurements of star positions, and most importantly the maps of the upcoming 4,126-mile ocean journey, maps which were in his head. The mutineers hadn't allowed Bligh any paper maps so he had to rely on his memory, proving the concept that drawing things helps you to remember them.

Another reason they survived was Bligh's leadership. The mutineers had only given them food and water to last five days, so in order to eke out their limited larder for what he estimated could be a six-week voyage, Bligh instigated strict rationing. Each man would get just a quarter of a pint – 140 ml – of water and 60 grams of food – they had some ship's biscuits and pork, which equated to roughly 150 calories – every day. Their journey actually lasted forty-seven days; so how did they manage on so little, especially as whenever spirits really flagged – or optimism briefly grew – the men demanded more of both?

It soon became obvious that the water ration was impractically low and it was increased to three quarters of a pint – 420 ml – per man per day. They were also blessed in this regard by fairly frequent rainfall, and they had water kegs to store it in. One of the downsides though was being perpetually wet; another discomfort on top of the cramped, immobile conditions aboard their overcrowded launch. They were fortunate that their voyage wasn't under a beating tropical sun, but mostly grey skies and even fog, the lesser of the possible discomforts. To try to get their clothes to dry out quickly, Bligh had the men soak them in seawater, wring them out then put them back on. Because of the salt, the seawater evaporated more quickly than the fresh rainwater, and so their clothes dried out faster. This was just another example of his leadership; his single-mindedness may have got him into trouble on the *Bounty*, but it was a strength here, where strict discipline was key.

To try to get more food, Bligh headed to one of the first islands where he thought the natives were friendly, Tofoa. Unfortunately, while initially benign, once the locals realized that the foreigners were without backup they became very anti. One of the crew was killed by stones, launched at them as they left with just a few coconuts and bashed breadfruit to show for their attempt to extend their rations. After that, Bligh realized the risks and didn't go close to islands again until he reached the Great Barrier Reef off Australia. He used a coconut to make a set of balance scales to eke out their meagre food equally, using musket balls for measuring weights. I think his leadership style was so successful because all the rationing was done with equality and fairness, but also with a verbal contract; Bligh got all the crew to agree to do it before they began. Whenever there were appeals, and sometimes begging, for a little more, he reminded them of the contract and the consequences – dying before reaching their goal – of breaking it.

They also tried to supplement the rations from the sea but it was a long time before they caught their first fish. Easier pickings proved to be seabirds – boobies – which could be grabbed by the legs when they landed aboard for a rest. They were then divided up and eaten, innards and all, by the ravenous crew.

I'm sure that they managed to last as long as they did in part because sitting still in a cramped space for twenty-four hours a day burns the absolute minimum of energy. There was bailing to be done as water splashed in, and being at sea always means you use your muscles to counter-balance the movement of a rocking boat, but the men in the *Bounty*'s launch were pretty static. Bligh devised a routine of frequently swapping places in the boat to at least try to stretch out stiff muscles and avoid painful cramps or seasickness, but by the time they arrived in Australia after a month in the launch they could barely walk, and the first man ashore collapsed.

But I think the real key to Bligh's survival was that he was a cartographer, a maker of maps. The fact that he'd been doing this for over ten years, and that he'd been to this area already, added up to him having a great mental map of the region by which to navigate; his charts were all in his head. All he used then was his compass for direction, a sextant to gauge his latitude – how far south of the equator he was – and a small pocket watch to work out his longitude. Knowledge of his 'mental chart' was enough to compensate for this last item's inaccuracy; he could sail west until he reached Australia, then go north and through the straights to Timor and rescue – he saw the route when he shut his eyes. Bligh's cartography continued during their ordeal; even while they sailed their little launch ever westwards he jotted down coordinates and made sketches of undiscovered islands for future Admiralty charts. As a leader, there really is no better way of navigating than knowing by heart where you need to get to.

Leadership is a huge topic and there are many books written on the subject, but I want to offer a very boiled down, essentialized take on how it relates to the principles of survival and self-reliance we've looked at. I think that the best leaders are able to help us connect what we do every day with the very biggest of our goals. As the author and consultant Simon Sinek has put it, they start with *Why*, not *What* or *How*.[32] By doing this they offer something that people can engage with at the level of their deepest goals and passions. As we've covered, survival situations have a kind of supercharged 'why' that everyone has bought into, but the best leaders are able to amplify that and stop those around them losing hope, maintaining their team's motivation. Bligh was able to consistently find ways to get the crew to buy into what they were doing, find tasks for them to feel they were active and keep them focused on their shared goal – getting home.

Studying survival stories, again and again, we see how good leadership is especially key in times of crisis, but it's important to recognize the immense pressure it puts on leaders and everyone around them who are looking to them for guidance. Just compare the men in the jolly boat with those in the outback in Chapter 4. When leadership weighs heavily on one person, it can be enough to make them jump out of the boat; when it's shared around, it can get them through almost anything.

It's relatively easy to be a leader when things are going well – to articulate what the organization is doing and why. But under adverse conditions, it becomes even more important to remind people why they do what they do. A really simple example is the tendency to cancel any traditional company parties as a classic cost-cutting exercise when times are tough, but in my book, that's the equivalent of inviting the ship's engineer over the side with you. If you're in that drifting boat, you need to be able to articulate why what you're doing matters and how it's going to get you rescued. Under the most immense pressure imaginable, that shared hope of achieving the goal broke down for all but two of the men in the jolly boat in Chapter 4. Whereas the collaborative and skill-based approach to leadership that the three men in the Australian outback took meant that they all contributed when their skillsets were needed.

It doesn't have to be the person with the highest social or hierarchal standing who leads a group, be they a hastily formed working group or survivors. Very often the best thing a leader can do is to trust in the competence of those around them and empower them to lead tasks.

Remember that Frank was initially able to inspire the other two men by his efforts. But then it was George who came up with the drills on the raft and Phil who found the fresh water when they needed it. A key part of feeling in control is feeling competent. Let others do what they're good at. If you need to help them, I've found that there's no quicker way to removing someone's enthusiasm for something than micromanaging them in how to do it. Try to ask questions that help them come to the best way to tackle it themselves. After all, if they never learn to do it, you'll end up always having to stand over them, whereas if they learn it themselves, you'll be able to use that mental energy on something else.

And finally, fairness is absolutely key. Bligh was scrupulously fair in making sure that reward was equal for all with his coconut shell and musket ball scales. As we've seen, for us to be able to maintain the sense of hope that we need to best accomplish difficult tasks, we need to be able to see how what we do contributes to the bigger picture. If we have a leader who allows credit or praise to be unevenly handed out to the extent that we no longer understand how what we do impacts the reward, we'll quickly lose motivation. What we need to do is keep on developing our ability so that we all contain our own leader.

Summary

→ Avoid self-inflicted isolation: if you can, keep people around you and prioritize time with others. In survival situations, having others around to raise your spirits can be key to maintaining hope.

→ Praising effort instead of talent instils a 'growth mindset'. An individual with a growth mindset will accept ownership of an issue. Once you accept that an issue is within your control you can then correct it with more effort; and it can be controlled.

→ Research from the emerging field of enclothed cognition has shown that the right clothing, whether you're going up a mountain or down the high street, will affect your confidence. Knowing you're in the best clobber for the occasion will improve it; and your performance.

→ In group survival, try where you can to only say constructive things to others, and remember to avoid as much as possible the 'mood hoovers' that might be inhabiting your space; they will have double the negative effect on your morale than the most upbeat person can raise it. There's no point fighting with pigs; you'll get covered in shit and they will just enjoy it.

➜ If you are feeling low, hack into the positive muscle–nerve feedback loop and hold a pencil in your mouth crossways. Your brain will think you're smiling and before you know it you'll be back to normal.

So now we've got the basic principles of survival; but how do we remain flexible enough to use them in the varying situations in our own lives? For that, we need to take a trip to the Arctic.

Chapter 6

THE IMPORTANCE OF LEARNING TO ADAPT

In 1845, Sir John Franklin led a Royal Navy expedition to explore the last 300 miles of uncharted Arctic coastline. He was fifty-nine years old, an experienced officer who had been present at the Battle of Trafalgar, and this would be his third trip back to the Arctic. It was an extraordinarily well-equipped mission. Franklin entered the Northwest Passage with 128 men in two specially designed ships, HMS *Erebus* and *Terror*. Both vessels were packed with the very latest Victorian technology, including retractable rudders and propellers, steam engines which powered heated cabins, a water distillation machine that let them produce drinkable water, and that most modern of inventions – several years' worth of canned food, plus porcelain plates and silver cutlery to eat it with. Franklin thought that he could 'make them spin out seven years' at a push.[33]

The weather was particularly unforgiving during their

voyage; they were icebound for longer than anticipated. Instead of making progress to the west, during the summer of 1847 the sea ice didn't break up at all. Stuck fast in the same position for much longer than anticipated, illness began to take a grip and on 11 June Franklin died.

We now know the innovative cans that their food supplies were preserved within had been soldered together with lead. The lead had gradually been contaminating the food inside the cans as it touched the soldered seams. As this poisonous metal accumulated in their bodies, the sailors' physical and mental health began to deteriorate. At the time lead poisoning wasn't well understood; the symptoms that the dying sailors exhibited were misdiagnosed as scurvy, the malnutrition disease that had dogged mariners for centuries. Scurvy is caused by a lack of vitamin C, which can be found in fresh food like fruit and vegetables, but less well known is its presence in fresh meat, which is why the Inuit could live in the Arctic and avoid the illness. Unfortunately for Franklin's crew, prevailing wisdom at the time held that canned goods were a cure for scurvy, so the lead poisoning patients were inadvertently administered even more poisoned food. By April 1848, they'd been eating from leaded cans for three years, and twenty-four men, one in five, had died. Those remaining had to make a decision.

Franklin's remaining men decided to leave their icebound

ships, their tiny specs of empire in a frozen world, and prepared to travel as the Victorians knew how. They used the
ships' boats as containers for tents and supplies – the ship's
carpenter attached oak sledge runners and the men hauled
the 600 kg-plus lumps over the frozen sea. The carpenter
also added brass screws to their boots to give more traction –
getting a load that weighs over half a ton moving requires a
good grip on the ice. They headed south, towards the Back
River on the Canadian mainland. The nearest outpost there
was over 1,200 miles away at a Hudson's Bay Company trading post called Fort Resolution. Although they had some
warm clothing made from caribou and seal fur, Franklin's
men didn't adopt the Inuit's best practice of building snow-
homes and hunting, reckoning that there was little to be
learned from the local 'savages'.

Franklin's crew used coal for heat – their then ultra-
modern ships had been fitted with steam engines to help
force a passage through leads (open channels in the sea
ice). But coal takes up a lot of space and weight if you're
pulling it in a sledge, whereas seal fat can be procured
with your next meal if you know how to hunt. They
would have had candles too, but in an uninsulated tent
candles are far less warming than they are in a cosy snow
shelter.

As Franklin's remaining crew continued man-hauling
their huge loads southwards towards the North American
mainland, they camped in their tents to rest before moving

off again. The men were already ill when they started out and so the physical strain, after months of relative inactivity on the icebound ships, was brutal. For rations, the fuel that powered all their bodies' efforts, they dragged their lead-soldered cans in the heavy boat-sleds.

In 1848, with no word from Franklin's party since August 1845, search and rescue expeditions were organized. We know that Franklin's men thought that others may look for them because they left a note in a cairn – a pile of rocks – at the point on King William Island where they dragged the boats ashore. Inuit also mark significant areas with stones – theirs are piled up to look like a human form and are called 'inukshuk', normally marking important waypoints or hunting grounds. I've found that any tall landmark helps navigation in a monochrome world where the cold, clear air makes depth perception and picking a route difficult. Maintaining direction up in the Arctic can be tricky too; the magnetic North Pole (where compass needles point) isn't at the true North Pole (where Santa lives at the top of the globe). It's actually several hundred miles from there and moves a few miles each year.

Franklin's men started to succumb to the combination of exertion, cold, scurvy and lead poisoning. At first, sick men were hauled in the boats, but as more and more emaciated sailors dropped from the towlines a hospital tent was erected and they were left with provisions, only eighty miles from their start point. It's difficult to imagine how that must have felt, but physiologically we can be fairly sure that having lost most of their insulating body fat they were in a poor state to endure lasting cold. Shivering is our natural defence to the cold, it's an involuntary reaction once we stop working and don't get into something warm, be that a suitable shelter or more clothing. Shivering is actually tiny spasms in small parts of our muscles, firing off slightly out of time with each other in opposing pairs at a rate of about ten to twenty contractions per second. This muscular movement doesn't generate as much heat as exercise, but it does raise our bodies output from 100W – the amount emitted from an old-fashioned lightbulb – to around 500W. This, unfortunately, all demands energy from our bodies. After the energy is used up, shivering stops, and if no food is eaten this can happen in as little as seven hours. Once that happened the men in the hospital tent would have begun to inexorably cool down. One by one, as the wind snapped at the tent canvas, they began to die.

Further south, the rest of the crew struggled on down the western shore of King William Island. Their decision to leave the ships and aim for the trading post 1,200 miles away on the Back River was made in the belief that it was their nearest hope of rescue; self-recovery. Unbeknown to them, one of the several relief missions that were sent to their area, led by James Clark Ross, managed to get a sledge team to within 200 miles of the ships. Hindsight is always 20/20, but had Franklin's crew chosen to send smaller, lighter teams towards the north, the direction from which help was most likely to come, and placed prominent cairns with messages giving their actual location, the story may have been different. As it was they were 'all in' on walking themselves out; this was now their only card and they'd gambled all of their lives on it. No trace of the sailors was found for a decade.

The importance of humility

So far, much of this book has been about preparing, planning and equipping ourselves with the right set of flexible principles we can use in multiple scenarios. But the story of Franklin and his men should stand as a warning never to become arrogant about what you know. What can seem like the best information at the time can turn out to be tomorrow's lead-sealed cans. However much we try and minimize the truly unexpected, we must always be prepared to update our tactics and behaviours when new information comes in.

One of the fundamental things I take from Franklin's story is that we can't allow our biases to stop us taking in good information. They ignored the evidence in front of them of how the Inuit people survived and thrived in that environment because they saw them as primitive and their own technology as superior. If I'm ever approaching a situation in life in which I get any kind of impulse to doubt or ignore the experience of someone who has been there and done it, I just remember Franklin and his crew. My advice would be to try and develop a healthy suspicion of things that feel 'too obvious' among a group of like-minded people. What we try and do, when discussing something in relation to our training plans, is to build moments where we cross-examine whether our solution is the best, or whether it's our brains taking shortcuts again. This can be as simple as going through the advantages another approach might hold in detail. We 'red team' any proposed course of action, with some of our group deliberately taking on an adversarial perspective. If the concept survives this ordeal then it has potential for development into an actual plan. If you can build it in, always explore at least one alternative when it comes to big decisions.

I'm not suggesting that someone could have turned around a situation like the entire Victorian attitude towards other cultures with the right question in a meeting. But I've found that keeping in mind that we could be the equivalent of Franklin and his tea sets is a wonderful reminder to take a moment to pause and check your assumptions.

It's also important to remember that the only reason we know about what happened to Franklin and his men is down to someone who approached that environment in the exact opposite way.

John Rae

Many ships were sent out to try and find what had become of Franklin and his men, but the story of what actually happened was eventually discovered by John Rae; one of the men sent on a search mission by the Royal Navy. Originally working for the Hudson's Bay Company, Orcadian John Rae took a very different approach to Arctic exploration; he travelled light like the locals, hunting as he went. While other search teams came by sea, John Rae approached the Northwest Passage overland by snowshoe and dogsled. Rae worked with the Inuit when he met them, asking about routes and hunting, copying their igloos as his preferred winter shelter and covering vast distances on snowshoes. To get up into the Arctic to start his search proper, he initially travelled through wooded areas. The 'treeline' is the demarcation where the boreal forest, also often called 'taiga', stops. It's the northern limit of a huge coniferous forest, bigger than the Amazon rainforest, that encircles the top of our planet. Living above or below the treeline in the Arctic requires a slightly different set of skills.

In the frozen woods below the treeline, the trees shelter the snow from the wind and it stays soft, making it impossible to walk on top of it, as you can further north, without snowshoes. Rae made his own, in the same style as forest-living indigenous people like the Ojibwe. Without snowshoes, movement in soft snow is practically impossible; you sink up to your waist with every exhausting step. It's hard to quantify just how totally draining this is until you try it, so I ensure all our future Arctic instructors have a short go at it like I have, to really know how much of a lifesaver snowshoes are. Snowshoes spread your weight, mimicking the large feet of local wildlife like ptarmigan and Arctic hares, allowing you to 'float' higher up in the snow as you walk. This also allows you to hunt and trap local wildlife for food as you go. That's how John Rae travelled, on snowshoes that he'd learned to make himself, covering thousands of winter miles. I've been up to the museum of his hometown, Stromness, to see his snowshoes; they're very slim and light – ideal for extremely long journeys.*

Here he was taking direct notice of the Inuits' adaptability. They cover vast distances easily, often using dogs to pull their few possessions on light sleds made from frozen fish and animal skins, with runners made of ice and moss. They found their food as they travelled, harpooning seal at their breathing holes in the pack ice, and larger animals like caribou as they migrated seasonally.

In his hunt for Franklin and his men, Rae stayed below or on the treeline for as long as possible, and then began to

---

* And about as far away from Victorian porcelain tea sets as you can get.

push out into the barren lands of the tundra. After many tough expeditions, in 1851 he eventually found the first remnants of the missing men – just two bits of wood with ironwork still attached – on the west side of the strait across from King William Island. No other search parties had found a thing, and it had been concluded by the Royal Navy that Franklin and his men were lost forever. But then, in early 1854, Rae was up to the east of King William Island when he encountered some Inuit. One of them was wearing a gold cap band. Rae asked where he got it and he replied that it came from the place where the 'dead white men' were. The man was vague about the location, and Rae knew it would still be deep under snow at that time of year. With some of his team struggling in the conditions he did what he could; he bought the cap band from the man and said that if anything else from the white men was brought to his winter camp, he'd buy that too. By spring he had amassed fifteen relics with identifiable markings, including a silver plate belonging to Franklin, and importantly, more verbal details on what had happened to Franklin's men.

So, what did Rae discover? The Inuit told him that south of King William Island, at the mouth of the Back River, other hunters had found about thirty corpses, some in tents and others under a boat which had been overturned to make a shelter. Rae's private report back to the Royal Navy further detailed that, 'From the mutilated state of many of the bodies, and the contents of the kettles, it is evident that our wretched countrymen had been driven to the last dread alternative as a means of sustaining life.'[34] This claim of cannibalism, based upon the second-hand testimony of local hunter-gatherers, was leaked publicly, causing outrage in Victorian Britain. 'Society' closed ranks against Rae, undermining his spotless record by vehemently refuting his report, and badly damaging his reputation as a result. But the words of the Inuit hunters were finally borne out by archaeological work in the 1980s, when human bones with knife marks consistent with butchery by metal blades were found on King William Island.

I can't think of a better example of what groupthink and closing yourself off to the best on-the-ground information can do. As we've covered in Chapter 5, our ability to listen to people not like us or with differing opinions is especially important in everyday life. The negative impact when this sort of narrow thinking becomes entrenched can be huge. It's been estimated that of around 1,000 personnel – many from the United Kingdom's Royal Navy – that pushed into Polar regions in the 1800s, 700 died. Seven in ten people who set foot on the ice.*

Having said that, sometimes learning to adapt doesn't just mean taking the information that others have supplied, but it means innovating and building on that knowl-

---

* See, it works doesn't it?

edge to create new solutions. To explore that, we can travel to an environment about as far away from the Arctic as you can get.

Bagnold – desert survival

For as long as we've had recorded history, accounts have been passed down about soldiers suffering in waterless landscapes. Even the word 'desert' has a strangely military etymology; it's from the Latin *desertum* – something that is left waste.

Deserts can be beautiful spaces, coloured anywhere from burning reds and deep purples to dazzling white, through all the yellow-ochre tones in between. And once you get away from the modern light pollution of our cities, their huge skies display uncountable stars during the cooler respite hours of darkness. Vast empty spaces like deserts have always attracted our imaginations; wondering what lies beyond their wide horizons kindles a sense of adventure and exploration.

This scale of emptiness is what drew an English Army officer called Ralph Bagnold into the vast deserts of North Africa in the 1920s. He was able to explore more than any previous soldier because he harnessed and adapted the very latest technology, developing techniques in desert travel that are still used by militaries around the world to this day.

It was Bagnold's sense of adventure that first compelled

him to drive a Ford Model T into the dunes of the Sahara. He was doing this in his spare time, spending his weekends traversing sand seas with fellow eccentric explorers, rather than drinking repetitive pink gins in the officers' mess and fleshpots back in Cairo.

Desert travel depends on water. Prior to the invention of the internal combustion engine, deserts were explored on foot or hoof. The people who live there know where the water sources are and use them as islands of succour, moving from one water point to another. So if you are truly exploring uncharted spaces of blank map you need to carry water with you. This is how armies before Bagnold traversed deserts, but the animals that carry the soldiers and their water need to drink too, and that limits their range.

Only fifty years before Bagnold set off into the Sahara, there is an account from the desert of north-west Texas of a group of US Cavalry soldiers who were lucky to escape that arid region alive after just eighty-six hours. While tracking an Indian raiding party, the horsemen became lost in the featureless terrain and, after an agonizing torment of thirst – during which they resorted to cutting their mounts' throats to drink the horse blood – they finally stumbled back to their original starting point by an alkali lake. A search party had been sent out and guided the last stragglers towards the water, but four of the forty men died. Their entire horse-powered operation unravelled in the arid desert heat in a little over three days; it was front page news at the time.

Camels, the ships of the desert, can carry heavier loads

further in hot conditions than horses, but even they have a limit of approximately ten days before they have to drink. Camels conserve water by making big changes in their body temperature, heating up as the day does rather than sweating straight away to maintain a lower temperature. If the desert gets too hot, and their body temperature rises to around 42°C, they've reached their maximum in terms of heat storage and they too will begin to sweat. Then later, as the sun sets and the night cools the desert, a camel will emit the heat it's stored up during the day, all the while minimizing its loss of water to the environment.

Increasing our range

In terms of exploration of desert regions, for generations we as a species were limited by the range of domesticated camels, until the petrol engine allowed us to go faster, further and carry more water.

This is precisely the opportunity that Ralph Bagnold recognized, as he whiled away his army posting to North Africa in the 1920s. He saw that in using a car to visit the less accessible ruins of ancient Egypt there was, 'an excuse to imagine that in those unfrequented, unsurveyed expanses of sand and rock there might be something still to be discovered just a little further out, and an excuse also to indulge in the newly-found excitement of driving a car where it was said cars could not go.'[35]

By learning from a couple of earlier pioneers, and by his own trial and error, Bagnold developed vehicle-borne desert exploration from a hobby into a science; he successfully adapted the right modern tech to centuries-old challenges.

The Sahara that he began to explore is a huge desert, equivalent in size to the subcontinent of India. Its interior contains flat gravel plains and huge sand dunes, salt flats and high rocky cliffs, but at that time no metalled roads. The one constant feature on Bagnold's daylight expeditions was the high, unremitting sun.

Back in the 1920s the only air conditioning that his cars had was made by removing windows and panels and driving fast. In an attempt to make some shade, the actual car roofs were left on but other than that the Fords were as open as possible.

Nowadays, millions of people commute every day through deserts in air-conditioned cars and jeeps with UV-protective tinted windows, stopping and calling for a recovery truck if they have a problem. There was no desert search and rescue back in the 1920s, and no expectation of others risking their lives to come and save those whose adventures had become misadventures.

One of the founding principles of Bagnold's explorations was that there should always be enough people and vehicles in the team to enable self-recovery should something go wrong. So Bagnold and his colleagues always travelled in at least two vehicles, and took passengers to help with navigating and pushing if their cars got stuck in the many areas of soft sand.

This, of course, meant that they needed more water. So they carried enough to drink and drink only; no washing or shaving – plates and cups were cleaned with dry sand. Working out how much water was enough was done initially by trial and error, including one notable miscalculation when Bagnold and another army officer only took one bottle of beer on a day-long expedition, and had to resort to drinking their car's radiator water. But by pushing their limits and increasing their knowledge they began to develop a set of principles for desert travel; carrying more than enough water is now a keystone piece of advice to anyone driving in desert regions, be that on or off road.

They became like vets for their vehicles; getting to know each one's idiosyncrasies and also knowing how to fix mechanical faults themselves; self-reliance personified. Bagnold even devised a way to make their cars waste less cooling water, by adding a separate water tank to the engine's radiator, thereby letting the heat dissipate into a bigger volume rather than overheating and boiling off into the desert air.

As for supplies, they always carried double their needs, so that if some unforeseen obstacle should bar their arrival at a town or fuel point they had enough petrol, water and food to go back the way they'd come. It wasn't long before journeys of a thousand miles became possible. They were pushing further and further out of what everyone else considered a comfort zone, but they were actively managing and reducing the risks as they went.

That's the best way to tackle any new challenge, in any environment. Gradually test out the terrain on the other side of your comfort zone, and build on the new discoveries you make. By making repeatable progress, building upon what you've learned, you'll find that you'll end up far further out than you thought possible. But always remember that it's an iterative process. Like with diets or exercise regimes, there's nothing as likely to cause you to lose heart as leaping ahead too far too soon. Keep things sustainable.

Bagnold and his team were driving into areas where no one had been before; there were no maps. His vehicles were made of steel, so magnetic compasses weren't reliable. In one further feat of improvisation and adaption to this new environment, Bagnold invented a brand-new navigational tool, the sun compass. It was a circular card that was mounted horizontally on his car's instrument panel. Sticking up from its centre was a small, straight, vertical metal wire. The shadow that the sun cast from this metal stick, the sun compass's 'gnomon', could be kept on a constant area of the circular card when the car was driven on a constant bearing. Bagnold calibrated these cards to correspond to the sun's position; provided it was updated every quarter- or half-hour as the sun moved through the sky, all worked well.

So well that it's still a NATO stock item for desert vehicle navigation to this day.

By knowing how far they had travelled and on what head-ings, they were able to fill in the blanks on the maps of their day. In order to conquer the final internal barriers – ridges of parallel sand dunes that are hundreds of feet high and block the route west through modern-day Libya for hun-dreds of miles – Bagnold let some air out his tyres and drove at them fast. Partially deflating his tyres gave them a bigger, squashed surface that didn't dig into the sand as much, and as long as the temptation to slow down was resisted a car could make it to the top of even the biggest dune. The real trick, learned through practise, was in slowing down in time for the top, or the car would be catapulted down the far side and could finish off upside down.

I wanted to include Bagnold's story because I didn't want to sound too loud a note of caution with the Franklin story. It's true that we must be careful that we pay attention to the way that other people do things, but that doesn't mean we should only do things the way they do it and stifle space for creativity. I think it's key here that Bagnold's initial connec-tion to driving in the desert was one of simple pleasure. He wanted to get out and see more and more of the desert but also to have an experience for no other reason than enjoy-ment. When you combine that with a meticulous set of goals, then all sorts of things start happening.

Crucially, Bagnold began with a mischievous approach to things and it's this that I try and carry through whenever I'm looking at solving a problem. It can be useful to think what your equivalent of letting down the tyres would be in a situation. Ask yourself the question – what would be an unexpected thing we could do here that could make a difference? It's especially important in my world, where we're working with such tried and tested ideas that we don't stop trying to innovate. And as you'll guess, I'm a big fan of encouraging people to represent information visually, to come at it from a different angle and use different parts of their brains.

What we need to do is find a balance between the openness of John Rae to the experience and knowledge of those peoples who came before him, and of Bagnold applying a new technology in a way that locals wouldn't be able to conceive of.

As I've highlighted throughout this book, what I want to try to do is reduce the burden on the thinking part of our brain as much as I can, so that we can free up the space to actually problem solve the things we should be concentrating on. If we plan, prioritize, increase our ability to get things done, then we open up the possibility of having the time, energy and attention to do what Bagnold was able to do.

And this is not just about efficiency. I think that exploration, moving from familiar ground to new areas, is beneficial to us in many ways. These days there are no blank spaces on our Google Maps left to fill, but we do have gaps in our personal experiences that offer an opportunity to explore. Pushing our own limits, even if that means simply travelling to a favourite or known spot by a new and different route, will increase activity in your brain's all-important prefrontal cortex. You'll be taking your brain on a growth journey. Journeying 'outside of our comfort zone' is a well-used metaphor. What lies beyond it is varyingly called the 'stretch zone', the 'groan zone' or the 'growth zone', but whatever the label, the curiosity that leads minds to wander into new spaces is what fuels new discoveries and enables growth.

Study of the human genome has highlighted a mutation of gene DRD4 that has been labelled in the media as 'the explorer gene'. Variant DRD4-7R is carried by roughly 20 per cent of all humans and it has been linked to curiosity and restlessness. Not having it, however, is no barrier to stretching yourself with a little adventure now and then. It's discoverer, Yale University evolutionary and population geneticist Kenneth Kidd, thinks that our behaviour is much more complicated than the press would have us believe. 'You just can't reduce something as complex as human exploration to a single gene,' said Kidd in a recent interview, 'genetics doesn't work that way.'[36] So don't be afraid to try something different, it isn't a simple case of being either hardwired for adventure or not – there's hope for us all to get out there more.

Returning to Egypt by accident in 1940, Bagnold managed to persuade the commander in chief there to allow him to continue his desert driving, this time with weapons. He formed and led the Long Range Desert Group, crossing the dune fields west out of Egypt and successfully attacking targets so far behind enemy lines in Libya that they were thought to be invulnerable. He had gone from hobby explorer to the developer of the tactics and techniques that spawned modern-day special forces.

Bagnold's hunger for desert knowledge and discovery wasn't limited to the grand scale. He studied desert sands down to the individual grain, researching how dunes formed and moved with time and wind. His study was so groundbreaking that it remains unsurpassed, and his formulas have been used by NASA in their calculations to explore other planets; they've even named giant dunes on Mars after Bagnold. Now that is what I call taking 'putting your name on the map' to a new level.

Here's one of my favourite examples of creative solutions to survival and real-life problems, drawn from a different desert on the other side of the globe.

Fog Catchers

To the west of the Atacama Desert of Chile lies the cold Pacific Ocean. By day the high sun heats up the ocean and fresh water evaporates into the sea air. At the same time the sun heats up the desert until it's hotter than the sea. This makes the dry air above the land rise faster than the denser wet air over the sea. As the hotter air above the desert rises the moist sea air offshore is drawn inland. Just like geography class at school. By the end of the day moister air replaces the dry air over the surface of the Atacama.

Deserts may be super-hot during the day but they can also be really cold at night. As moist air cools down overnight it can't hold as much water. The point at which an air mass runs out of water storage capacity is called its dew point. Below that temperature the water condenses out of thin air to form dew and fog. By morning in the Atacama huge banks of fog are created along the coastal strip – the locals call it the 'Camanchaka'. That's a lot of fresh water to be had in a desert region, if you can collect it.

So how do you harvest fog? Fog is just tiny beads of water suspended in the air. Those beads will stick to anything cold that they touch, so when I was doing some survival training there we hung up pieces of parachute from the rock faces, like the sails of a small yacht. At the base of these upside-down triangles we placed our water bottle cups, with the point of the triangle of parachute material leading into the cup itself. By morning the parachute material was damp all over, and the many tiny rivulets of dew were running down them into our metal mugs.

The technique can be so productive that a village up the coast gets all its water that way. In Chungungo they hang up seventy-five plastic mesh sheets, each twelve metres by three metres and looking like big volleyball nets, with a small gutter at the bottom leading into collection barrels.

Each sheet can take 150 litres of water from the sky per day. The Chungungo villagers are known as the Fog Catchers.

Summary

→ If you can, allocate a small portion of your planning time to 'red teaming' your proposals. Nominate a part of your team to behave like reasonable opposition, in order to find any weak points in your strategy, and then counter them by making the right adjustments to your plans.

→ A blend of approaches will normally get you further than sticking dogmatically to one way. Be open-minded to how the 'locals', the others that are already successful in your field, tackle the issues you are facing. Don't carry porcelain tea sets into the Arctic.

→ Travel as light as you can, but always take enough resources, or means of getting them, to enable you to get out again.

→ Catch fog. Be creative – if what you need doesn't exist use local knowledge and adapt it to make a novel solution to your needs.

→ Don't edit out ideas that seem too far-fetched when you're forming early answers to problems. Bagnold was

able to delay the attack on Allied forces in the
Second World War partly because he decided to
try letting his tyres down to get further.

→ Whether or not you carry DRD4-7R, there is always more
to be learned over the next ridge, so have a look.

So we've seen the importance of flexibility and how to work
with other people. Now it's time to add the final layer of
complexity that is unique to military survival; how to do all
this when you are operating in a place where the inhabitants
are trying to catch you out. Let's look at the benefits of
evasion.

Chapter 7

TUNE IN

Over the last few years, I've been lucky enough to travel through some of the most extreme environments on the planet. Today though, the sun is shining and I'm sat on a quiet stretch of drystone wall in England's Lake District, admiring the view. The view in question isn't the anorak-flecked, heather-covered peaks behind me; I'm looking at the edge of the woods three metres away across a single-track country lane.

The very same view captivated a young man eighty years ago. His name was Franz von Werra. When Franz gazed onto this shadowy treeline in the autumn of 1940 he was admiring it because of what it represented to him: freedom. Just a month earlier, Franz had been flying his Messer-schmitt fighter plane for the German Luftwaffe in the Battle of Britain. He'd been shot down over Kent and he was now a prisoner of war, being held three miles up the road in

Grizedale Hall in Hawkshead. And because we Brits are such good sports, Franz and his fellow captured pilots and U-boat crewmen were allowed to go out, under guard, for a walk in the fresh air every other day.

That's what I'm here to do today during my spare time – minus guard: retracing the route Franz took once he'd escaped from his hosts. I'm sat looking at the same terrain through an evader's eyes, on the exact spot where he rolled over this wall to escape, and trying to imagine what his options were back then. I thought a lot about freedom as I wrote this book.

I've been teaching British pilots how to evade from the enemy if they get shot down for most of this century. Evading is a level of complexity up from just surviving in a harsh environment like a desert or the Arctic; doing it when the very people that inhabit the harsh place are also against you. At the very least they dislike you, and they want to get their hands on you. If the desert island's isolation leads to a desperate need for human contact, then surviving in the territory of your enemies is the polar opposite. People in enemy territory are to be avoided. In this scenario you not only have to address the survival priorities – what will kill me first – in relation to your physical needs, the area's terrain and weather conditions, but you must also add to that list the task of avoiding being detected by people that actively want to cause you harm.

What motivates people to endure the hardships of escape and evasion? Consider the alternatives. There's an oft-quoted truism in military survival training; that 1,000 days spent evading are better than one day spent in captivity. I think of the skills that survival helps us sharpen as freeing us from captivity.

As I sit in the sunshine, it strikes me again that what survival does is essentialize things we all take for granted. What Franz kept in his mind every day was how important it was to get back home, to see the people he loved. So many people spend their working lives with their motivations for what they do unclear. It is a kind of privilege to be insulated from the essentials of survival, but it is also a kind of hardship. Though we are unlikely to ever achieve Franz's clarity of purpose, I think we should all try and keep in mind the reasons why we do what we do. It can be easy to sink into cynicism about the jobs we do, the lives we lead, rolling our eyes and shrugging. But what I've found studying the stories of those in this book is a reminder of that flame that burns in us. That desire to stay alive, to go back to our lives. I wonder about whether those that did survive, when they got home, found themselves able to slip back into their lives, or whether they were forever reaching for that certainty, that purity of experience that they encountered when everything non-essential was stripped away.

I think of those motivated by duty. Hiroo Onoda, a Japanese soldier, evaded capture after the island he was on – Lubang in the Philippines – was overrun by American forces in 1945. He hid in the jungle of the small island's interior, maintaining his sense of duty and obeying his original orders not to surrender. He eventually came out of the trees to his former commanding officer in 1974, still carrying his officer's sword and service rifle, which he'd maintained in the jungle for almost thirty years.

I think of Dale Zelko, John Colter, Lance Sijan and the well of motivation that allowed them to do what they did.

I know a little of what Franz must have been thinking, and following his lead I drop from the wall and start moving.

As I enter the woods opposite Franz's drystone wall I immediately feel a sense of security. The trees here aren't tightly packed, yet there is an instant envelopment, distancing me from exposure to the field of view. Franz escaped in the early afternoon; it would be several hours until sunset and darkness enabled him to move across the many areas of open ground that exist up here. He used the four hours of daylight he had to move through the big woods of Grizedale Valley. That's what I'm doing now, following the animal-like instincts that we all carry in us somewhere to move slowly and thoughtfully, using the terrain to stay concealed from view.

Looking down as I carefully place each foot, I notice the telltale signs that another person has walked this way. There's a twig, broken in two places with about a hand's-width distance between the breaks. People in shoes break twigs like that when their flat soles step on them. Further on, I see a boot print in the edge of some mud. Suspicion confirmed, plus I now have a timeline for their walk too;

there is no sign of raindrop marks on the print. It rained last night so I know they walked here this morning.

Poachers and gamekeepers have played a high-stakes game of 'cat and mouse' for centuries in our woodland. A poacher's life could depend upon their ability to avoid detection; they would instinctively avoid stepping in soft mud. Taking deer from the English King's 'New Forest' was punishable by death, the lesser crime of disturbing his deer resulted in blinding or having a hand amputated. Avoiding detection was a skill worth investing some time in, and would be learned from an early age. A key part of moving through a landscape undetected is going slowly and pausing regularly to 'tune in', allowing all your senses to soak up ambient environmental information. Sight is just a part of the evasion picture. But you can only do this if you've got the key principles of survival locked down. One of the benefits of the principles is how they encourage us to take in as much information as possible. When you start, it becomes a way of life. One of the gifts I get from the job I do is the amount of time I spend in nature.

The myriad bird calls in woodland all tell a story about what's happening around me. Lots of birds are territorial and change their call to one of alarm when people approach, so if you've stopped to tune in and you hear birdsong change at a distance there's a good chance that another person has triggered the alarm.

Similarly, birds like pigeons will fly away noisily from

their treetop branches as you walk below and disturb them. So if you enter a quiet wood and no pigeons noisily evacuate, it's fair to assume that someone is already in there. Pigeons can also give your position away in open ground; they always avoid flying over humans and will normally make a sharp, obvious turn in mid-air when they see one below in the countryside.

The Romans used birds, specifically their alarm calls, to military advantage even earlier; geese make a huge racket if they are disturbed, so the clever Romans knew when their positions were being infiltrated by the honking it triggered. Some whisky distilleries in Scotland still use geese to patrol their warehouses.

I think about the current fashion for the term 'mindfulness', for stopping and noticing, for paying attention to what your body and mind is telling you. I know how some of the survival instructors would react if I told them that we're basically practising mindfulness every day. I probably couldn't print that reaction, but I still think it's true. A lot of what we do when we're out and about could be labelled as mindfulness; we're paying a lot of attention to *now*, to what's around us and the many senses that our environment is firing. We're on a continuous, multi-sensory scan for threats and opportunities; the feel of the ground beneath your foot, a smell of smoke, the breeze on one cheek, the sound of snapping twigs. You have to be 'in the moment', dialled in, to be able to absorb this information.

If you want to heighten your sense of hearing while you

stop to tune in, there are a few tricks you can employ, the kind that poachers use automatically. Because of the way our heads are constructed – an internal system of tubes and cavities containing air and fluids – your eardrums will move more freely if you open your mouth slightly. That means your ears will be more sensitive to small vibrations in the air, and that is what sounds are made from. This can be further tweaked by turning other, more distracting senses off, and the easiest way to do that is to close your eyes. That will focus a lot more mental energy onto what signals are coming in through your ears. If you then want to determine which direction a sound came from, slowly moving your head side to side – as though you're listening to a politician – will make it easier for your brain to compare the two sets of sound waves arriving at your two ears. Once your brain knows which ear is further from the source, it also knows roughly the direction it came from – it's a bit like using your ears in the way a radar dish sweeps for electrical pulses.

Try it in a meeting; eyes closed and with the slightly open mouth and head sweeps. It can be informative and guarantees that others will want to know your thoughts. More useful than closing your eyes to hear more is actually freeing up your ears, especially in potentially hostile environments like busy city streets that you aren't familiar with. Taking out the ubiquitous earbuds or removing headphones at places like road crossings, where you need that extra touch of situational awareness, can be an actual lifesaver.

Poachers also knew that any noise they made could give

them away, so they learned to place their feet carefully. If you need to move through woodland quietly, there is a balance to be struck; softer ground makes less noise – to a point – but leaves more sign of your passing for gamekeepers to follow up later. So placing feet down slowly onto firm ground is the answer; and the way poachers do it is by gently putting the heel down first, then rolling the outside of their foot's sole down until their toes are on the ground too. This avoids the slapping sound that a boot sole can make if it's allowed to flap down straight onto the ground. And if there are areas of ground covered in potentially noisy dry twigs or leaves, they are just avoided or, if that's not possible, the poacher's foot is placed down slowly, sweeping the brittle debris to one side just before their weight is allowed onto it.

If making a footprint in soft ground was unavoidable, poachers would make the tracks they left behind them look more washed out by putting their shod feet into grain sacks and tying these at their ankles. This removed the hard, fresh edges of the sign they created, making the footprints look a lot older; creating a 'colder' track for the gamekeeper and one they would be less likely to follow with any urgency. And the poacher would be sure to check that the things they were carrying – like lamps, nets, poles or snares – weren't going to knock against each other noisily as they moved. They'd be tucked away in a pouch or bag to cause minimum disruption until the time they were actually needed.

Where I'm walking, in the Lake District wood that Franz von Werra escaped into, I stop to tune in to my surroundings. I know from his memoir that the goal he'd set himself lay in the west – the coastal towns where he hoped to stow away on a boat to neutral Ireland – and getting there meant climbing the wooded slope ahead. Our eyes are drawn to movement, so to avoid that, Franz would have chosen a route through these woods that meant he was out of sight from any forest labourers, in what we now call 'dead ground'.

This best evasion ground is in the dips and folds of terrain that place you completely out of sight, like the re-entrants that get carved over millennia by mountain streams. Looking ahead there are several of these, and one is leading west. I'm sure he would have evaded this way, it's the best cover available, so I follow his instincts up the hill.

I feel the warm April sun shine through the trees onto the left side of my body. It's rising north of east at this time of year, but always sits due south at midday, which is where it is now; acting as my compass. In the northern hemisphere the sun will rise in a progressively more northern part of the horizon until our longest day of the year, late in June, when it rises in the north-east. In those weeks you'll get sun pouring into areas of your home that don't normally receive it, making you draw the curtains as it sets in the north-west to avoid seasonal reflections on the TV screen. That's because our planet's axis is slightly tilted, and in June we are tilted towards the sun more than at any other time of year.* The further up our planet you go in June, the more pronounced this effect is, meaning that inside the Arctic circle the sun is visible for twenty-four hours; it never sets. Down in the southern hemisphere they are tilting away from the sun, so their days are shorter – it's winter – and in Antarctica the sun won't rise above their horizon at all. So it's only at the equinoxes, those days of equal light and dark in March and September, when our axis is pointing neither at the sun, nor away from it, but is sideways on, that the sun rises exactly east and sets exactly west. Not a lot of people 'know' that, but we've all witnessed it. When you start to pay attention to those kinds of little natural details you really start to tune in to the world around you, and keep track of time.

Think green

Going to an open, green, outdoor space is beneficial in itself. A recent study found that if a city neighbourhood has more trees in it, even just those that we pass on the street, then that area's residents will feel more well and healthy. It's the equivalent effect of a 20k boost to your earnings.[37]

---

* It's tilted at 23.4 degrees, if you ever have to answer the pub quiz question.

In the many recent attempts to quantify the restorative powers of immersion in nature, scientists from around the world have measured all manner of variables, up to and including our brainwaves. One area of research is the seasonal variation in the amount of the natural 'happy chemical' serotonin that we produce. Serotonin is used to transmit signals between our nerve cells and, because the availability of it in our system has a direct effect on our mood, it has also been used in therapy for depression. It has been found that serotonin is lowest in our system when we have our lowest exposure to sunlight, during the winter months. Further research has even shown a significant correlation between the average number of hours of sunshine and the rate of 'completed suicides'.[38] In short, getting outdoors is good for your mood, and if we know that it is likely to be lowest in winter and early spring we can make a little extra effort to get some sun therapy during those periods.

Knowing what we've just learned about the Earth's tilt, and knowing that each day the Earth spins once on its axis, we can turn our lunch break in the park into a deeper connection with the rhythms of nature. Above the Tropic of Cancer in the northern hemisphere's temperate zone, where most of us live, when the sun reaches its highest point in the sky at midday it is directly to the south of you – because of the Earth's tilt. So by doing nothing other than eating your sandwiches and observing the sun or its shadows, you have just added episodic memories to semantic ones, and thus formed a truly autobiographical bit of useful orientation knowledge. And why is finding south without a compass useful? Well, it's the sunny side of any hill for picnics, and it's the part of the sky where the fixed search and rescue satellites sit, so it's a good direction to call for help. If you live in the southern hemisphere, below the Tropic of Capricorn, delete south in the above and insert north and the principle holds for your temperate zone too.

Nature – whether you are just looking at pictures of it or spending several days 'unplugged' in it – is very good for lowering stress, reducing negative 'ruminative' thoughts and improving that all-important executive-attention function of our brains. People have recognized this for years, it's just that now empirical science is catching up. Back in the time of Queen Victoria, at the dawn of the modern urban-industrial era that we now inhabit, the English nature writer Richard Jefferies wrote:

> I restrained my soul until I reached and put my foot
> on the grass at the beginning of the green hill itself.
> Moving up the sweet, short turf, at every step my
> heart seemed to obtain a wider horizon of feeling.
> With every inhalation of rich, pure air, a deeper
> desire. The very light of the sun was whiter and
> more brilliant here. By the time I'd reached the
> summit I had entirely forgotten the petty circum-

stances and the annoyances of existence. I felt myself, myself.[39]

That captures it quite nicely. And that's the next step in developing your own positive feedback process – walking through the green spaces nearest to you, your natural world.

But Franz wasn't just enjoying the weather, he was actively evading those looking for him.

The other cover that was available to Franz in the autumn was tall bracken, not yet above ankle height in the early spring of my walk. In the October of his escape it would have been an almost chest-high extra layer of concealment, but it would also be dead and brown, rustling noisily as he threaded through it. It would also have added to the 'sign picture' that he was leaving; not only marks on the ground from his feet – 'ground sign' – but bracken bent and folded in his direction of movement up to chest height – 'top sign'.

Franz had got a good head start on his hunters. Because of the disruptive actions of his fellow prisoners the alarm wasn't raised until they had been marched for around a quarter of an hour back towards the camp. He was further aided by what happened next.

After realizing they were minus one prisoner, the guard sergeant turned his horse and galloped back to where the group had been halted when Franz got away. The sergeant then spurred his horse into the woods in a frantic and unmethodical search. All he achieved was to obliterate any tracks left by Franz, either ground or top sign, making any follow-up by dedicated trackers impossible. If you don't know which way the person you're tracking is going, you have to cover all 360 degrees of the circle of viable directions.

Shortly after the sun set at 6.23 p.m., Franz was at the far edge of the big woods looking out over open, greying moorland. In those four hours his hunters knew that he could easily have covered 16 km, but because they hadn't been able to track him they couldn't be sure in what direction. That meant – using maths pioneered by Eudoxus of Cnidus in the fourth century BC* – they had a potential search area of over 800 km²; over 300 square miles. Had they known by tracking him that he was going west, that area would drop to a quarter of the size, but the sergeant's horse had covered his tracks, 'fouling' the sign.

Digital evasion

Most of the human predators at large today hunt online. It's the modern equivalent of a largely ungoverned landscape where we all leave digital footprints and open avenues for the unsa-

---

* That one from school: a circle's area is equal to Pi multiplied by the square of its radius. Clever Greeks.

voury to exploit us from afar. A few simple things can help and they don't take long to do, just a little worthwhile extra effort.

Start by checking the privacy features of any social networking site you're on and then make sure that only the people you choose are able to view your details. Get a stronger P4ssword than the obvious ones – weak ones are like leaving your front door key under the mat these days – and try to remove personal info such as your home town from your username.

Don't post pictures of where you live if random strangers can view them, and whatever you do don't post real-time holiday photos or dates when your home is going to be empty. Burglars these days do a lot of their recce online. It's not as hard as you think to take these few protective steps and they make you less likely to fall victim to online or offline crime; go to your social site's security advice page to find out exactly how.

Once you've made yourself and your important data safe by checking your security settings, consider taking a physical break from your digital self; even a short one can be beneficial. Research has shown that the psychological pressures of maintaining an airbrushed version of your persona online is inherently stressful. Not only could you strain your cheek muscles by puckering for too many selfies, but you can actually hurt your brain by constantly worrying over how others see you.[40]

So why not reap the benefits of not constantly checking the quantity of little pixel thumbs and hearts you get by downloading a social media blocking app? They can be activated for set chunks of time so that you can go off-social-net without having to go completely offline. That way you can have the internet without all the distractions and subtle, yet real, stresses of social media.

If you'd like to know what kind of footprints you're leaving there for the uninvited to follow, look up something like the service provided by the University of Cambridge's 'Apply Magic Sauce' tool. The kind of digital breadcrumb trail that you unwittingly leave online can be used by anyone from market researchers and advertisers to burglars. Tools like Apply Magic Sauce let you view your social media presence more objectively, while simultaneously letting you know how much of *you* you're showing, ensuring that in future you only post the details that you're happy for others to use.

Better for your health still is to turn it all off and go out into a green space for some fresh air and a walk. If you like taking photos, just put your phone into airplane mode instead of turning it off. Your brain will love you for it, especially if you read a printed book instead of an e-reader, and use a paper map to navigate there rather than a small screen.

These days, if someone goes missing in the hills, one of the first things to establish is their intended route. The best thing to do if you're going out in a remote zone is to let friends know where you're headed and when you expect to be back, before you go. It narrows down the area you're missing in – and therefore speeds up any search activity – if you get into trouble and can't raise the alarm yourself.

As he lay in the edge of the woods looking west at the open ground he would soon have to traverse, Franz watched the sky change. Tuning in to your environment also involves looking up; doing so here it lets you see the future, by forecasting the weather.

What Franz saw was cloud cover higher up that was rapidly followed by more and more cloud at lower and lower levels until the sky became totally overcast. This is a sure sign of wet weather coming in, and if you can spot cirrus or 'mares' tails' – high-altitude wispy clouds that are formed from a thin layer of ice crystals – they are a long-range indicator of changing weather. Once you see a high formation that looks dappled like fish scales, you're seeing cirrocumulus clouds – 'mackerel skies' – and that usually means an approaching low-pressure system; bad weather. There's an old rhyme that is a good way to remember it: 'Mares' tails and mackerel scales make tall ships lower their sails.' Laying in the wood's western edge, Franz felt the first drops of rain hit him. It wouldn't stop raining for over a week.

Tuning in to the sky and its weather lets you do more than just forecast it, it helps you to navigate. If you know where the prevailing wind is for a region you can use its effects on the landscape as a compass. Franz had a small escape compass, but they can be hard to use in the dark, wind and rain, plus the wind itself was giving him a steer. In the UK, most of our weather comes from the south-west; that is our prevailing wind direction. The storm that Franz was about to get soaked by – a Lake District valley, Borrowdale, recorded 80 mm of rain the day after he escaped – came in from that area too. So keeping the lashing rain on his left cheek as he walked, overcoming the instinct to turn away from the bad weather, would ensure that he kept moving westwards towards his goal, however unpleasant it felt.

The longer-term effects of our prevailing winds over many years will also create shapes that can be read by evading airmen at night or hillwalkers anytime. Trees growing in exposed areas – like the uplands of the Lake District – will have been moulded throughout their lives by the prevailing south-westerly wind to grow away from the gales; they are pushed more towards the north-east here. The tops of coniferous trees like the ones at Grizedale, the very tips that grow above the wind-breaking effect of their neighbours, have all been sculpted to the north-east too.

If it's very windy the effect can be even more dramatic. I was out evading at night on my survival instructor course on Dartmoor, which has very similar terrain, when the winds were so strong that mature pine trees were being blown over. Row upon row of massive compasses, all pointing north-east. Their giant windblown root bases and stumps are still visible there to navigate by, over twenty years on.

As the weather came in and the sun set on Franz in 1940, the colours faded from his view, until finally the world turned into the shades of grey that we associate with the black and white films of his era. Night adaption is the name for the process the human eye goes through as ambient light levels drop after sunset. What we witness is a change in the way colours appear – reds and oranges get darker, greens and blues become lighter grey, until they all form a kind of pixilated greyscape. What's actually happening is that the two types of light sensor at the back of your eyes are changing shift. 'Cones', the receptors that we use during the bright white light of day, are clocking off as it gets darker. The more sensitive 'rods' that we use during the low light of night start coming online. Rods don't detect colour, hence the gradual shift to monochrome that you see. It takes your rods about five or ten minutes to fire up, and they won't be fully up and running for about half an hour.

Franz would have waited until his eyes' night adaption was complete before breaking cover and heading out from the woodline onto the open moorland. The weather may have been awful but that is an advantage to a hunted person. Evaders know that they are likely to be more highly motivated to endure it – and therefore work harder – than any unimpressed conscript soldier who's been drafted in to search for them. Plus the sheets of rain that lashed the area would wash away his footprints and form a curtain that obscured him from view. He would still need to be cautious though, because even on a rainy night, the sky will be brighter than the land. And Franz was on high ground, so there's a good chance at this early point in his escape that the hunter force would be approaching his area from lower down in the valley. They would be ascending towards him, and if he didn't stick to the dead ground of small streams and contours to conceal himself, he would be silhouetted against the lighter sky to the hunters below.

Going out for a walk at night can give you a completely different reading of an area that's familiar by day. What is very familiar to you by day may appear alien once the sun has set. Because new experiences are good for stimulating our brains, a night walk is a beneficial brain workout. An added benefit is that you don't have to necessarily go somewhere totally new to do it, just somewhere safe. If you can get away far enough from the ambient cultural lighting of towns on a clear night, there's another tool you can use to keep yourself orientated as you move: the moon.

How to navigate using the moon

The moon will change shape over the course of four weeks but if it's up when you're out there's a good chance it'll range in shape from a waxing – getting more full – crescent to around the familiar circle of a full moon. These are the phases of moon you'll see between 6 p.m. and around midnight, but if you're a real night person – out walking in the wee hours – you'll also see the waning crescent.

Whatever shape the moon is when you see it on your walk, it can give you a bit of orientation help, and the simplest technique to remember is also most easy in mid-latitudes, the region midway between the poles and the equator where most of us live. If you live in the northern hemisphere and you can see a crescent moon, draw an imaginary line between the tips of the crescent down to the ground. The point where your line meets your horizon is roughly south. Once you know where south is on your mental compass, you know where north, east and west are too.

As we saw with the sun earlier, this method works in the southern hemisphere as well, but your line finds north.

And as we also saw with the sun earlier, because of the way our planet turns on its axis, the moon appears to travel across our skies from roughly east to roughly west. Because the moon only appears bright by reflecting the sun's light, its shape shows where the sun's light is coming from. If you know that the sun recently set in the western part of the sky and you see a half-lit moon, the bright half will be facing the western sky. Also, just like with the crescent example above, the shadow line between the light and the dark side of the moon will still run towards the southern horizon. This is good to know because you can often get a quick glimpse of the moon in a partly cloudy sky, where there's not enough cloud gap to orientate by the partially obscured star constellations that flit in and out of view.

Franz's views of the moon would have been fleeting too, as the bad weather clagged in during his night-time trudge across the moors towards the western ports. But he maintained his determination and his route, even though the cold rain was lashing him mercilessly. As he continued west across the boggy moors the ground began to gradually drop away again.

Even in a sparsely populated area, avoiding people isn't easy. The lay of the land meant that contact with them was almost inevitable. The Lake District was carved out by glaciers, grinding their way down from the north in the last ice age; Arctic charr still inhabit some of its lakes. So the terrain he was crossing from east to west was an obstacle in itself; the glacial valleys all ran north to south there. That meant that he would have to cross the valley bottoms, as he couldn't get west if he stayed on the empty moorland 'fell' tops, and people live in valleys.

Glacial valleys are flat-bottomed and the ones Franz had to cross all had rivers in them too. He had to pick a route across them and all their inherent obstacles, knowing that the army and police would also be patrolling the valley floor's main roads; yet another barrier. As well as roads, the valleys are also criss-crossed with mile after mile of dry-stone walls, and as farmers or soldiers passed them they would be sure to notice any disturbed stones or muddy boot marks – 'transfer', in tracking terminology.

The flat fields also had livestock that could betray his presence; sheep would scatter from him when disturbed and inquisitive cattle would be likely to run over to investigate him. Both of these reactions would draw the attention of any soldiers out on patrol or watching from high points. The rivers would be in spate after all the recent rain, so wading or swimming was almost suicidal, but any bridges would likely have had guards on sentry once his absence was known. If he tried to use the smaller bridges that farmers have on their property he would risk waking their dogs, whose barking would lead to a light coming on in the farmhouse, and phone calls to the local police . . .

So Franz rested by day, at least initially, and only travelled after dark. The later at night that he travelled the better; it gave people the chance to fall deeply asleep in their cosy farmhouses and the hunting patrols to become thoroughly soaked and under-motivated in the cold, wind and rain.

For the next three nights, Franz successfully avoided all human contact and left no sign to indicate his presence or direction of travel. The search area grew and grew, making it harder for the army and police to effectively cover. The BBC and national newspapers published his description; the whole country was now on the lookout.

Through following his steps and putting this together with my previous experiences, I know a little of what it must have felt like for Franz. He'd been out in the worst of northern England's elements for three days and nights with no food other than some windfall apples. He must have been close to hypothermia, if not already suffering from it. Pushing your mental and physical limits in bad weather while being tracked and hunted gets more and more difficult as hours turn into days. Little things that you do to save energy, but that each time risk detection or capture, can become habits when you're exhausted. It takes supreme self-discipline to maintain the harder yet safer option, rather than the riskier shortcut.

Even if it's cold and you're soaked through, it's too dangerous to light a fire for warmth when you're trying to avoid being found. There are ways of hiding flames but fires always make some smoke. A strong smell can be equally indicative of a person's presence as the sounds they make, and if the conditions are right it can travel further. Even when you move away from the source of the smoke, its smell gets absorbed into your clothing and that will linger at any still-air site you stop at long after you leave.

By forcing the lock on a small stone hut, Franz gave his hunters the first confirmation of his presence in three days. All of his hard evasion work was undone by one cold, tired shortcut. The two Home Guardsmen who'd spotted the broken lock opened the door and shone their lamp inside. A gaunt, wet, pale face squinted into their bright light. He looked like a broken-down tramp, and they soon had him tied at one wrist with twine. They began to lead him down the steep, slippery hill towards the army trucks parked in the valley below. If they got him down the hill it was all over. Franz knew as much the moment he spotted the trucks way below. Timing his move to coincide with an awkward patch of ground, Franz pulled hard on the cord tied round his wrist, overbalancing the man who was holding it like a dog's leash. As that guard fell, his lamp went out and Franz forced his way past the other guard, running uphill into the wet night. This man followed, but like many Home Guard volunteers he was old, and he also lacked Franz's key advantage; a burning desire to be free.

Franz had managed to regain his freedom, but the shortcut of seeking shelter in a remote building had cost him dearly. The massive pool of resources that had up until now been spread thinly over the whole of the Lake District and northern England were soon focused onto this one small valley. The odds were now stacked on the side of his hunters. They knew an exact start point for their search, and by drawing a line to it from his initial escape point in Grizedale, they knew what his direction of travel had been. By then extending this line on their maps his destination goal of the west coast was obvious.

His lack of evasion security discipline had been much more useful to his predators than leaving the odd footprint or broken twig had been.

Over the next thirty-six hours, hundreds of civilians, soldiers, policemen and their dogs combed the valley. At just after half past two on the afternoon of 12 October, Franz was spotted. He had been flushed from the woodline by a huge line of searchers during daylight, and a shepherd spotted him higher up the hill as he crossed a stone wall. Our eyes are drawn to things by day for a few reasons, movement being the most obvious one. Franz was far away, but the shape of his body going over the wall was enough to be picked out, as it was silhouetted against the sky: 'skylining' being the cardinal sin of evasion.

By the time the troops and locals had made it up onto the hilltop and crossed the wall onto the bleak open moorland beyond it, Franz had vanished. The hunt leader organized his troops and police into a straight line and once again they set off on a fingertip search of a barren landscape. The shepherd who'd originally spotted Franz and raised the alarm hung back with two other locals and scratched his head in disbelief. All those trudging across the empty bog in the rain now muttered that he'd been mistaken or had had one too many pints with his lunch.

They'd walked off some distance before the shepherd spotted slight movement in some coarse grass only a few metres away. It was in a damp area of ground that the line search had already passed. He ran over and his feet sank deeply into the boggy patch. Then he spotted a pale face in among the taller grass; arms, legs and feet were submerged in the bog, blending their shapes, shadows and silhouettes with the mud. He'd almost stood on him. This time Franz was handcuffed before being marched back to custody. Via the pub.

There are so many reasons for us to feel under threat in the modern world. Twenty-four-hour rolling news with ever more scare stories about the dangers of modern life, our endlessly chirping smartphones which mean we can never truly escape. I think the principles of survival can ultimately help us evade this. They can open space in our brains for us to remember what's important, remember what is fundamental and what is unnecessary.

Franz von Werra's adventures in the great outdoors didn't end on the Lake District fells where I followed in his footsteps; persistence and perseverance are keys to long-term success.

A couple of months later he escaped again, this time by tunnel from a different camp, and bluffed his way out of a police interview before summoning a lift in an RAF car to the nearest military aerodrome. He was in the cockpit of the very latest RAF fighter about to get his engine started by groundcrew to fly home when he was re-arrested. Not long afterwards he was shipped to Canada, where he promptly jumped from a train into deep snow and made for the border with the then neutral USA. After enjoying the limelight of New York for a time, he moved via German diplomatic channels through Central and South America to

Italy. He remained the only German who managed to escape from the western Allied mainland and returned home to fight again.

On this bright spring day, as I retrace his steps, I can see him in my mind's eye, walking out across the fields, his pursuers long behind him, travelling light, travelling fast, free.

Summary

→ Because the inside of your head is a complicated system of tubes and cavities, if you want to hear something faint, like a conversation about you in the next booth, open your mouth slightly to allow your eardrums freer movement, and close your eyes to focus.

→ Taking out the ubiquitous earbuds or removing headphones at places like road crossings, where you need that extra touch of situational awareness, can be an actual lifesaver.

→ If you're going out into a remote region let friends know where you're headed and when you expect to be back, before you go. It narrows down the search area if you have an accident – and therefore speeds up any help getting to you if you're unable to raise the alarm yourself.

→ Cirrus clouds, also known as 'mares' tails' – high-altitude wispy clouds that are formed from a thin layer of ice crystals – are a long-range indicator of changing weather. If you see a high formation that looks dappled, like fish scales, that's cirrocumulus clouds – 'mackerel skies' – and that also usually means bad weather. Remember the old rhyme: 'Mares' tails and mackerel scales make tall ships lower their sails.'

→ It takes your eyes' rods about five or ten minutes to fire up when it's dark, and they won't be fully up and running for about half an hour. What you'll notice as you try to look at something close up in the dark is that the centre of your vision – where your cones work – is a blurry 'blind spot'. So to see something close up more clearly in the dark, look just to the side of it and bring your rods into play. If you want to avoid losing all your night vision, close one eye when something bright, like a car's headlights, approaches.

→ Avoid assisting hostile humans online: don't post pictures of where you live if random strangers can view them, and whatever you do don't post real-time holiday photos or dates when your home is going to be empty. Burglars do a lot of their recce online.

→ Break out from your cell (phone): studies are mounting up that show our increasing dependence on apps and satnavs is reducing our ability to navigate without them.

As well as navigation, learning some simple survival skills by practicing them before you need them, even just knowing how to tie a couple of basic knots, means you won't have to reach for your smartphone to have the answer with you.

So now we've completed our tour of the Survival Triangle, the motivational feedback loop of PLAN → Work →Hope, and the things that can support it. How do we make sure that we use it? How do we move towards what Maslow described as 'self-actualization', going beyond self-esteem and satisfaction in everyday tasks? How can we use the Survival Triangle as a key to unlock our full potential? The secret to this is in the survival instructor mindset of continuous learning. And for that, we need to go to the jungle.

Chapter 8

WIN OR LEARN

On 15 February 1942, after over two months of conflict, the Japanese Army captured Singapore and precipitated the largest surrender of British-led military personnel in history. Around 80,000 people became prisoners of war. A handful of British soldiers managed to evade capture and hide in the jungle. One of them was called Freddie Spencer Chapman and he lived as a fugitive in the jungles of Malaya for three and a half years, all the while being hunted by the Japanese Army. Freddie also attacked the roads and railways that his pursuers were using while he evaded, and he set up several covert jungle training camps for Malayan resistance fighters; all under the noses of his hunters.

Even better, when he wasn't working on that, he was observing and recording the flora and fauna of the area, for submission to the Royal Geographical Society and Kew Gardens back in the UK; planning ahead for a long-term peacetime future.

I believe that what set Freddie apart from other Brits who stayed behind after Singapore was captured – because initially there had been several small groups – was his attitude to the environment and its hardships. He witnessed first hand the effect that feeling oppressed by the surroundings had on some of his colleagues; how the close, fetid air and no glimpse of a horizon through the green slowly sapped their physical and mental strength. Several actually died; they just became more and more withdrawn as they sat and languished in their jungle camps, until finally all of their hope dissipated.

Not so Freddie; he had always been able to take the initiative and form his own plan in a situation that the other left-behind Brits were reluctant to even begin dealing with, mentally or physically. He refused to view his surroundings, his predicament, as a hopeless trap. He wasn't so naive as to think there were no hazards in his jungle; he wasn't unrealistically optimistic, but neither was he unnecessarily pessimistic. He summed his situation up perfectly when he wrote: 'It is the attitude of mind that determines whether you go under or survive. There is nothing either good or bad, but thinking makes it so. The jungle itself is neutral.'[41] We can recognize that as the perfect stoic mindset in which realistic optimism can flourish.

How did he cultivate this attitude? In what will feel familiar now, he learned it through repeated practise, by starting off on small forays away from home comforts when he was younger and building up to longer trips. He eventually went on Arctic expeditions, living and working with the local Inuit of Greenland, learning transferrable life skills by understanding what mental and physical hardships he could endure and those that others had endured before him. And he taught these skills to others before the war at Gordonstoun School. Prior to his own three-year jungle evasion epic he taught other soldiers too, quoting the axiom 'the best way to learn something is to teach it'. He never stopped learning, even while he was being hunted through the Malayan jungle by the Japanese Army; he viewed everything as an opportunity for growth. As Nelson Mandela said, 'I never lose. I either win, or learn.'

Going in

It's this aspect of Freddie I'm thinking of now, as I'm sitting in the back of an army helicopter with Tommy, looking out of its open doors at the green carpet of Borneo jungle far below. Tommy is a very experienced army jungle warfare instructor, and between us we're about to run the UK's jungle SERE instructor module in, what is to us, a brand-new area of Borneo's unspoiled forest. The people we teach here will go on to teach others, and one day what they learn could save their lives. I'm thinking about the importance of this, but also thinking about how I want people to use this book. Not read it and put it back on the shelf but to make it part of their lives. To use its stories and ideas as part of their learning and teaching every day. Because, like Freddie Chapman, the act of learning and teaching are inextricably bound up in my mind.

Below us, it looks like someone has dropped a piece of glistening coffee-brown ribbon onto the carpet, and my eyes instinctively follow, as it wriggles away towards blue-green hills on the far horizon. The cab is moving at two miles a minute, and as we reach those hills the ground rises up gently to meet us. My newest group of instructors are almost at the end of their training journey, and I'm about to set up a jungle base camp for the final module. It still amazes me how quickly helicopters complete journeys that in the past were measured in footsore weeks or months. The green carpet now becomes more detailed – in a familiar but perfect analogy – like a field of broccoli tops.

The helicopter's skids settle onto the small, red-brown landing site surrounded on three sides by huge jungle hardwood trees, the kind with buttressed roots that look like rocket-ship fins. It's the only flat area big enough for a helicopter to land within miles, perched on the side of a steep ridge overlooking a crumpled sea of green.

Before we can teach them how to survive here, before we can dispel common myths and build their knowledge, we have to check out the suitability of this site. So, before the cab comes back with our base camp set-up gear, we need to check that this bit of forest has what we need – a reliable source of drinking water. We know it has everything else – jungles are full of natural resources that we can use to address the other three survival priorities of protection, location and food – but we need to see that the small stream marked on our maps isn't dry.

Unusually for the time of year it hasn't rained here for a while; the waterways are low across the region. That's the paradox of being in a jungle; you're wet most of the time from sweating but water isn't always easy to find. In here you need a lot of water just to maintain one person, and Tommy and I need to supply a static camp of over twenty people for almost a month. So, we'll need to find a lot because we know we're all going to sweat a lot. If the elements ever become abstract and academic, ten minutes in the jungle reminds us of why we follow these rules. We're going to be following our PLAN, but not blindly.

Before we got out here, we went through what the worst-case scenarios would be, and a dry stream came top.

It's not a great plan to travel alone in remote places like this, so we're following our own advice, the 'buddy-buddy' system of keeping an eye out for your mate. If you are alone here even a simple slip on a muddy track can have serious consequences – as you'd expect there's no satellite phone reception under the thickest tree canopy – so sticking together is an easy way to reduce the risk of a small problem turning into a big one.

Jungle myths

There's a lot of survival bollocks spoken about 'the jungle'; the commonest being that it's a 'Green Hell'. Firstly, jungles are found all around our planet, they are intensely rich with life precisely because conditions inside are ideal to support it. Life thrives in jungles. There are many variations in tropical forest types and all are subtly different, but we tend to think of a singular 'the jungle' – the impenetrable, steamy green tangle of legend – and file them all into one mental pigeonhole; places to avoid. Jungles can be challenging in many ways, especially psychologically, but death isn't the foregone conclusion that a quick google of 'jungle survival' would have you believe. If anything, true, original, 'primary' jungles are much more at risk of being killed off by us humans than the other way around. But you have to arm yourself with information to see that.

Here we will teach many of the same things that Freddie Chapman taught more than seventy years ago. Because they work. But we'll also teach a whole load of new things too. Here we will have to deal with how to give feedback – constructive criticism – to people who aren't yet good enough at doing something we do. We're in the jungle pretty regularly but for many of them, this might be the first time they've ever been in this terrain. They're desperate to make a good impression; normally they're used to being the expert in their world. Often there's the danger that a desire to project aptitude can shade over into overconfidence. Here we will praise effort, not talent. It's something we're constantly on the lookout for in our world: complacency. Nothing will get you in trouble quicker than thinking you've finished learning.

Constant endeavour

I think about how Freddie continually looked for ways to hone his self-reliance skills, writing how 'to add some spice to life and at the same time practise myself in the difficult art of jungle navigation, I used to go out and deliberately get lost so that I was forced to use all my resource and energy to find the way home again.'[42] This is not something that most people would do voluntarily, but I think it's key. Chapman knew that in order to be ready for when it really mattered, he was going to have to test himself under real conditions. I want people who read this book to put its advice to the test in real conditions. Even if it's just getting into the habit of writing a list of things they want to get done that day on the train every morning. Even if it's just getting into the habit of imagining all of the many reasons a colleague might be in a bad mood and giving them the benefit of the doubt.

Finding your way through jungle, like any dense woodland, is very daunting at first; getting lost is a constant hazard. But not getting lost is a skill that is surprisingly easy to learn if you have a few simple tools – a map, compass and a way of counting distance – plus time to practise. It's the first practical lesson we give to the new instructors when they arrive at our jungle classroom, because they'll need the skill from day one. But it does take practise to truly learn, regardless of how much navigating in other areas people have done before, lots of practise. Through practise, the complicated threatening mass can be tamed and brought under our control, we can learn to look through it, not at it, and we can learn to live there.

As Tommy and I move down the narrow ridgeline to the area we're recce-ing for our base camp, I feel a sharp tug at my left arm and stop. A wispy tendril of vine is growing across our ridge-top track, this tunnel through the green, and I've brushed past it. Looking at it more closely I can see that it's attached itself to my arm's flesh – through my shirtsleeve – with its many pairs of backwards-pointing spiky barbs. This is the infamous 'wait-a-while' vine. To keep moving would create a series of nasty parallel tear lines in my shirt and skin. So I carefully hold the part that's attached itself to me, and pull it out in the opposite direction to the way it went in. A quick flick with my parang – the local type of long jungle knife that is always on my belt here – cuts the offending stem and clears the path.

Later I'll have my revenge; the soft growth inside the wait-a-while's tip is high in carbohydrate and features in my jungle food lesson. I smile – there couldn't be a better metaphor for how, with a little knowledge, a threat can be mastered and turned into an opportunity.

As well as being great for the vegetation, the humidity and heat here are also ideal for the growth of bacteria and other parasites. There are myriad microscopic opportunists just waiting for a breeding ground to pass by, and our bodies represent a lottery win to them. The warm, damp conditions accelerate these processes too, so any cuts, scrapes, bites or stings need to be dealt with quickly. Because I stopped moving as soon as I felt it latch on, the wait-a-while only left a small pair of scratches on my arm, but part of my routine tonight will be to check myself over and then apply an antiseptic iodine tincture to any and all small cuts that I find. This will hopefully prevent an infection over the coming weeks; it's going to be a war of attrition on my body, and prevention is better than cure. The jungle makes it vital to look after yourself at every stage.

That's why you won't see any of our training team waving their parangs around as they walk, like you see actors do in films. Big jungle knives like machetes and parangs have really long cutting edges, so they only come out when there's something that definitely needs to be cut; constantly swinging them in front of yourself here is daft and dangerous. Not least because of the risk of a self-inflicted parang bite, but also because any extra effort makes you sweat even more, and one of the biggest threats here to new arrivals is heat exhaustion.

At the foot of the ridgeline track that we've been following down from the helicopter landing site Tommy and I stop and listen. The vegetation is much denser here and the ground levels out for a few metres. Through the acoustic backing track of bandsaw beetles and van-reversing bird-songs, we hear the sound we'd hoped for, and stepping forward a few more paces, there it is. A small, sandy-bottomed jungle stream, flowing fast enough to fill our final checkbox. Green light: we head back up the ridge to pass the message to the distantly thudding cab.

Getting comfortable

Before long the rest of the training team and our equipment join us, and within an hour black ropes and olive-green tarps turn this little patch of forest into tropical-downpour-proof admin areas and classrooms. Smaller shelter-sheets and hammocks delineate personal spaces, a fire is lit to cook on; the jungle has become home. Soon it will be a school. It starts to rain.

After this first lesson we take the new instructors out into the local area on a long walk, and spend time every day afterwards honing the skill. It's good to keep a record while you're learning, preferably in a notebook, of where you've been; listing distances covered and compass headings followed, like mental breadcrumbs through the woods. There's enough going on without them using up mental energy on things they don't need to. And you can't always rely on a jungle map, nor is it always easy to know where you are on one; most of them were made from aerial surveys, so photographs of treetops were all they had to go on. This means that lots of smaller features below the tree canopy may not be on the map, and some things which are – like small hillocks – could just have been really tall trees that were growing many years ago, when the aerial photo surveys were taken. The jungle reminds us to make sure we have a healthy curiosity for whether the information you have is the best, and then whether you can get better information.

Wet and dry

In the evening, my soaking wet daytime clothes are removed and packed into a sealable drybag, which prevents anything crawling inside.* My jungle boots are inverted and each placed onto the top of a purpose-cut long straight stick that's stuck vertically into the floor, again to deter anything making their dark cave-like interiors home. I dry my feet and use foot powder on them, and all of the day's scratches and cuts get cleaned.

Then the one other set of clothing that I brought in, the

---

* Roll-closed at the neck, these watertight rucksack liners are invaluable when you go somewhere this wet.

dry set, is put on. It's kept for sleeping in, giving my skin some respite from the perpetual damp, a 'wet and dry' routine. And no matter how tempting it may be to keep the dry set on the next morning, I always put the ammonia-stinking, sweat-wet day set back on instead.

The first time you do that it feels wrong. Deliberately taking off dry clothes to put on smelly, damp ones is counter-intuitive. A reminder of how important it is to override our brains sometimes. I do it because I know that if I didn't all of my clothes would be damp; and that would make the cooler nights an ordeal. That brain again – always looking for the quick reward, unable to imagine the future very well. Once I'm dressed in fashionable wet, I bash my boots together to shake out any unwanted guests before putting them on, and finally my parang is fastened at my waist.

The forest floor terrain itself can be very demanding – a jumble of sharp-edged ridges, the way the landscape would look if you'd crumpled up a stiff paper map into a tight knot and then let it slowly unfold. Hard work to traverse when those ridges are hundreds of feet high.

This all adds up to slow progress – in some areas you typically have to measure your speed in terms of hours per kilometre, not the other way around. Whenever I move through jungle, I make sure that I stop regularly to drink. Normally on a long hike – like when I'm showing the new student instructors around on their first go – I make sure we stop every hour, for ten minutes. I take my pack off, sit down and open one of my water bottles for a good swig. The new instructors normally watch this closely – at this point they still smell of shower gel and are reluctant to touch anything, let alone sit on the floor. I know that by fully resting – even for just ten minutes – I'm giving my body, and those of the less-familiar new blokes, a chance to cool down. As we know, the way that we perform best is not by ignoring that we have limits but by recognizing them and making them part of our conscious process.

Iban pace

The local experts here, in the north of the island of Borneo, are called the Iban. We work with them because this jungle has been their home for generations, they are as comfortable here as you are in your living room. I soon learned to adopt the Iban's pace, minimizing sweat and accidents by moving steadily and taking the time to be more aware of my surroundings. I've adopted their saying of encouragement, 'Agi idup, agi ngelaban' – the literal translation is 'Still alive, still fight', but I prefer what my Iban friend told me it means while we were in the jungle: 'While I breathe, I hope.' There it is again.

Moving slowly, at Iban pace, is in itself a skill that's hard to acquire, especially for our new instructors who are keen to impress and press ahead. It's more of a mindset or attitude, and it takes time to switch down a few gears and pay more attention visually. You must continuously shift your gaze from immediate close focus on compass, thorns, or spider-webs to more distant general shapes as you select a route; observing the way the light patterns reveals ridgelines smothered in foliage. For me, this is the perfect analogy for how our brains want to take shortcuts when we think we're under threat. But if we slow down, take the time to get information into our systems, we can see that the right decision might not be the one we immediately went to.

It's a long process, but it is always the fastest way to make progress here, even though you move more slowly. Without taking the time, and care, to navigate accurately via a series of short legs to unmistakeable objectives, it is really easy to have a mishap or to become disorientated or lost; and then getting back on track will burn much more time, energy and daylight than going at Iban pace ever would have done. It's far better to pick a limited route and move forwards than to thrash around in lots of different directions at once.

So much of what we've covered in this book is about moving at something akin to 'Iban pace' in our everyday lives, so that we make the best possible decisions. If we don't, we will soon end up tangled in the undergrowth, caught on the thorns and wasting all of our energy needlessly.

For our new instructors' final exercise, we have them

dropped off by helicopter deep in the forest. Their brief is to navigate to a known friendly zone, but their drop-off spot is too far from that goal to be reachable in one day's walk. They have to overnight without any home comforts, using what's in their pockets to create hearth and home. These graduates are going to be military survival instructors, so it isn't just jungle camping and hiking that they'll be tested on. All kit is pared back to basics, and they have to move through the trees with a tracker force of Gurkhas trying to catch them. They'll be evading like Freddie Chapman, living and moving without leaving a trace. They will be tested under the most extreme pressure, and they should find that their knowledge stands up.

This is the feeling I want someone finishing the book to have, as if they've learned how to make camp in a jungle. To see that an environment that might feel threatening at first, in which we have no agency or hope, can be approached with knowledge and process, until it is just another environment for us to thrive in. There is no greater feeling in my mind than that of self-reliance, of feeling that regardless of what you have in your pockets or backpack, or whatever is helping you to extend your range, it's what's in your brain, what you are capable of doing, that really matters. It's my hope that my pupils will be able to impart that feeling to those they teach. Because as Freddie Chapman knew, the best way to learn is to teach, and the best way to be the best teacher is to never stop learning. It's our job to inspire them to pass this on to the men and women they will train, who in turn will feel more able to face whatever the world throws at them.

As we sit around a campfire that night, people talking about various things, there is a simple joy to knowing that whatever is likely to be thrown at us, the chances are, we'll find a solution.

Summary

→ Go at Iban pace when you tackle large projects: by progressing at a steady rate that minimizes but never completely removes stress, I know that I'll get to the finish line without having wasted any effort; like I would if I inadvertently followed a bad route because I rushed things.

→ Never believe that you know all there is to know about something. There's always more to learn if you look hard enough or ask the right questions.

→ The survival instructors who eventually perform the best take stock of what's not working, they focus on their faults, and work on them until they're corrected, not giving up until that happens. It's a technique known as deliberate practise.

→ A lot of the small hills on jungle mapping are just the sites where tall trees used to grow. The next time someone hands you a pre-written plan, ask yourself if the information that it was founded on is 100 per cent up to date. It will save you time, hopefully by avoiding trying to climb admin hills that aren't even there.

CONCLUSION

I'm sat writing this conclusion in the desert, but because of the human brain's ability to imagine what it's like to be somewhere that it has never experienced, you don't need to have set foot in a desert before to know how it might feel. I can describe it now to allow your brain and nervous system to remotely sense it – the dry heat, the salt on your skin. The air here is hot, it feels like the blast you get from opening an oven door to get out a pizza, but you're surrounded by it on all sides. The light is white-bright, so you squint and the creases that makes in your brow form little creek beds for the beads of sweat that you can feel trickling down your forehead. As well as being hot, the air is also crystal clear, things appear nearer than normal and you can see more detail in the reds, browns and yellows as you narrow your eyes to look.

In exactly the same way you just imagined how being in

a hot, bright desert feels, we can imagine how it might feel to be catapulted into a dire situation. Every day, someone in the world endures something that seems crushing at first. Armed with the ideas based on military survival skills that I've presented in this book, you can think about how you might use them to help in your tough moments, your daily trials.

The first time I was exposed to a situation in which I had to apply the skills we've examined wasn't that long after I'd completed my advanced RAF aircrew survival training course, and it came completely out of the blue. I don't remember the day – it was probably a Tuesday – that I got a phone call just after I'd landed. The distant voice on the phone said I was no longer allowed to be a pilot; medical stuff, everything's fine though, don't worry, but come over to the medical centre on the base as soon as you can.

At times like these, we have to remember that others have endured far worse, and that our minds are capable of solving all kinds of problems. We must also know that any rescue demands action from us; we can't just sit there wait-ing for it. Being armed with that knowledge, I acted; it was just after I was medically grounded that I signed up to become a survival instructor myself. I'd helped out at the RAF school during gaps in my flying training before, and it was something I'd planned to do later anyway. I now had an unexpected bit of time where I wouldn't be flying, so I thought why not use that ground time to my advantage and learn a new skill?

I changed my environment, from waiting to hear news at my home base, to pursuing an opportunity in the outdoors. This new field of work was fantastic fun, and I found it physically and mentally stretching. I was also seeing a new element of control over one possible direction I could follow – even if my flying career proved to be approaching a dead end, my alternative survival instructor hope candle burned on. It's become the most interesting area I could ever have imagined, a rare insight into mental and physical possibilities. I've been at it for over twenty years now and I still feel like I've only started to scratch the surface.

It's easy to fall into the trap of focusing only on the negative aspects of things that are out of your control. At times it can seem like you're being simultaneously assaulted on multiple fronts: medical / health; career / money; ambitions. But these things aren't out to get you – they're neutral – it's your responses to them that define threats and opportunities.

What I've found is that you can cope with anything that doesn't kill you. All you need to do is apply the fundamental principle underpinning everything we've looked at:

You can reprogram your brain so that you handle situations better.

You can change your brain in the same way that you can increase your body's physical stamina through light exercise. Your mindset isn't fixed, it's mouldable and you can decide how you shape it. This mindset training needs to be focused. It all demands a little *effort*, but the rewards and the freedom from hassle it brings are huge.

The key to maintaining effort – your perseverance engine – is knowing that by doing something to change your situation you will feel more in control of it.

Thankfully, being unexpectedly catapulted into a situation where the choices we make are life or death is an incredibly remote possibility for most of us. Even with the supposed spread of random acts of violence in our cities, the odds of you being subjected to one are vanishingly small compared to the far higher probability of a mundane – but more likely to be lethal – road traffic collision. As Dale Zelko the stealth bomber pilot perfectly proved, though, the fact that something is unlikely does not make it impossible.

Thanks to the ongoing research of psychologists and some survival instructors, we are continuously adding to our understanding of *why* we behave the way we do in life-threatening scenarios. It's only by understanding your hardware – the brain – and the ancient software that it's running, that you can foresee the types of scenario that you haven't yet programmed a 'patch' for. Once you appreciate the fact that there won't be enough time – even though it might only take around ten seconds – to develop a new plan on the spot during a dynamic event, you can start to produce them pre-emptively. A reminder: only *thinking* about what to do will help, but physically running through your actions – by walking the route to an unfamiliar hotel's fire exit, for example – will help more should you need to access the file for real.

Alongside this, now that you know what kind of chemicals your body pumps when it's stressed by a predator on the ancient hunting ground, you can use the right actions to dissipate those chemicals should they be triggered tomorrow by the thought of an important presentation or job interview. That type of anxiety will affect your mental performance if you let it, so interdict it by chewing gum, wearing the right outfit, 'power posing', or simply by breathing in a 'triangular' way.

We all have the latent capacity within us to be best-practice survivors. We can all alter the way we do things to improve our chances of performing to our full potential. The very process of applying those techniques to mentally and physically prepare for unlikely – but not impossible – worst-case scenarios will also increase your health and happiness by making you feel more comfortable in any unpleasant situations you have to endure. Be they in the wilderness or the workplace.

We are an incredibly tough species, infinitely adaptable, and by remembering some of the examples that I've shared with you here, it's possible to push yourself a little further when you have to. If you know what another human like Lance Sijan is capable of enduring, and then set yourself small, achievable goals like he did, you too can maintain your motivation to continue, one small step at a time. By sharing with you my Survival Triangle of Hope, PLAN and Work, and the reasons behind why it works for me and others, I hope you can use it as a walking pole – a support to lean against when your journey gets tough.

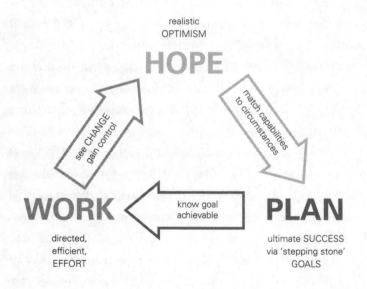

You can survive anywhere with the right PLAN. A fundamental understanding of our own vulnerabilities is vital to knowing what to do next. By prioritizing your actions with PLAN (**P**rotection from injury and the temperature of the environment, getting **L**ocated by rescuers, **A**cquiring water *then* food, and finally **N**avigation), the survival 'to-do' checklist, you are directly responding to the things that can harm you, in the right order. This is what makes you more efficient when you work at anything, and that buys you the most time possible, and time is the one commodity we'd all want more of if it was ever on sale.

What I've come to realize is that you don't have to be pitched into adversity to use survival skills. The lessons I've learned from teaching survival instructors have helped me to find my own way through a huge range of potentially unpleasant spaces, from my email inbox to foreign cities in rush hour. To get through anything you just need to tap into the techniques that have worked for others in their direst straits and then apply them to your own tea-cup storm. There are so many awe-inspiring survivor examples to choose from — the ones that we've looked at in this book are just my choice, the ones I find most useful. Now you can start to curate your own library of people at the edge of human existence, from scientists to astronauts.

We all have the latent capability to surmount surprise obstacles, to endure for longer than we thought we could, to triumph through a workplace emergency. The main hack in anything is to know that you have unused reserves – there's always a little more in your tank than you think, even if you feel like you're on Hope vapours.

The easiest way to retune your understanding of these

limits is simply to see more of your natural habitat. Once you reconnect with your natural environment and start really enjoying a bit more time outdoors, the painless process of increasing your independence and skills will inevitably lead you to stretch yourself further out of your comfort zone; into the fresh air of better physiological and psychological health. Even the simple act of taking a stroll to a park bench for your lunch has a multitude of fringe benefits. The stroll itself is at the right speed of movement to allow creative thoughts to propagate. Varying the route you take will expand the performance of your brain's all-important executive functions in your prefrontal cortex. Being in greener spaces will improve your feeling of well-being, and observing your surroundings and nature's interactions with them will help you to retune to your optimum environment, debugging all the e-stresses of our modern world in the process.

Making a little effort to push yourself out further than you'd normally go today will ultimately make you feel more comfortable, confident and self-reliant in any environment tomorrow, and that will make you feel less stressed. And no matter what they say on telly, stress kills more people than plane crashes, shark attacks and selfies combined. So relax; why not go out for a mooch?

APPENDIX 1
PRACTICAL ADVICE FOR COPING DURING A PANDEMIC

Show me a man who though sick is happy, who though in danger is happy, who though in prison is happy, and I'll show you a Stoic.

EPICTETUS[43]

Since this book was first published, I've been contacted by many readers who found its advice helpful in their daily lives and challenges, from those working in offices to members of the emergency services, and also everyday folk battling things like cancer and PTSD. Since the beginning of March 2020, readers have also reached out to me to ask for some practical advice that will help during the coronavirus disease (COVID-19) pandemic. I hope you find the additional material here useful.

John Hudson
March 2020

The shock of the new

Life-changing moments can happen at any time and any-where – not just in the extreme world. But life-changing moments can also happen more gradually and, as we've seen with the current pandemic, it can be no less of a shock when the realization comes. As we've seen throughout this book, accepting this and taking responsibility increases your ability to tolerate hardship and to restart your perseverance engine. This is the key to your survival mindset and one of the greatest skills to develop in life.

Know your enemy

If 'survival' means 'staying alive', viruses raise a fundamental issue because they themselves survive by leading 'a kind of borrowed life'.[44] By understanding what a virus is, we can make sure any 'borrowing' of our lives, or our loved ones' lives, as hosts is avoided or is as temporary as possible.

Viruses are small strands of genetic material that rely on infecting other living cells in order to reproduce.[45] Once in there, they build replicas of themselves and then break out of those cells to find lots more cells to repeat the process, either in that host's body or another one. When viewed under an electron microscope, we can see that their genetic material is surrounded by a ring of protein spikes which look like a crown – the Latin for 'crown' is 'corona'. It's these protein spikes that allow the virus to anchor onto living cells and infect them. There are many types of coronaviruses,[46] from the common cold and pneumonia to even more severe variants that attack the respiratory system. The corona family of viruses are carried by animals and can sometimes make the jump to humans in a 'spillover'. While several known coronaviruses are circulating in animals and have not yet infected people, the COVID-19 virus was first identified as spilling over to humans in late 2019 in Wuhan, China. After comparing the new virus's genetic material with 217 similar types, scientists in China think that this one made the leap from bats to humans, probably via snakes; bats and snakes were on sale at Wuhan animal markets.[47]

How does COVID-19 work?

The COVID-19 virus, or SARS-CoV-2, is transmitted by droplets, typically emitted when an infected person coughs or sneezes – a single cough can produce up to 3,000 droplets. The most likely path of infection comes from inhaling the droplets of an infected person's cough or sneeze. The modes of infection are being studied and, for the most updated information, I suggest you check the website of the Center for Disease Control and Prevention.

Once the virus infects a person, it can take days until illness symptoms occur, which is probably one of the reasons why COVID-19 has been able to spread so quickly and widely.[48] As some of the milder symptoms can appear like other seasonal illnesses, in order to diagnose that someone actually has COVID-19, a test called PCR (Polymerase Chain Reaction) needs to be done, which can identify the virus's genetic fingerprint.[49] At the time of writing, there is no specific medical treatment or pre-emptive vaccine available, just supportive care, but scientists globally are working round the clock to identify weaknesses in the COVID-19 virus, from how it attaches to our cells, through to ways of inhibiting its reproduction and spread.[50]

You can understand and adapt

Now you know how this particular virus spreads and works, you can fully appreciate the reasons behind advice that's given by professionals in disease prevention like The Center for Disease Control or the World Health Organization (WHO).[51] As we see in Chapter 5, with Captain

Bligh's successful crossing of over 4,000 miles of ocean in an open boat, when you know *why* you should do something, you're much more likely to stick to the right course of action and thereby achieve your biggest goals. This is why it is so important to always get your information from the most credible source of facts and guidance when you can.

Try to have more than one way to access information too. During large social upheavals, key infrastructure like power, internet and mobile networks can get overwhelmed. Your nearest TV transmitter is probably still working, though; why not check if you can still pick up its signal if all the streaming services stop? If all else fails, an old-school radio that runs from batteries will pick up news updates. There may also be a radio fitted in your car.

Know yourself – how to defend your vulnerabilities

The next step to dealing with a pandemic is to understand what practical steps to formulate in your own PLAN to stay safe. Regardless of the nature of the threat, the principles of survival remain the same. PLAN (**P**rotection, **L**ocation, **A**cquisition, **N**avigation – see Chapter 2 and Amelia Earhart's desert island for the full story) is still the key to your priorities in a scenario like a pandemic. That means the first thing you need to do is to run through the 'what will harm me first?' (where are the biggest threats?) questions. There is a huge role that taking responsibility for *personal* protection plays here. And, in the case of a pandemic, when you take the right steps to protect yourself, of course, you're also protecting others. In the case of COVID-19, humans are now the main vectors for this virus and an infected person may not display symptoms while unwittingly carrying the virus. This is why the WHO recommends,[52] wherever you can, to avoid 'agglomerations' – groups of other people and specifically also the kinds of places and venues where other people are closed in together.

If you have to venture into areas with other people, try to keep at least one metre away from them (but doubling this WHO advice to two metres whenever you can, as the UK Government suggests, would be even better). As important as this is, there's no need to be rude about this 'social distancing'. We are a civilized society and the grease that makes its wheels turn is good manners and mutual respect. We are all in this together, so smile because, in the long-term, the virus will pass, and we will get back to normal, and you wouldn't want to fall out with people over a perceived lack of good manners.*

---

* Remember that hack from Chapter 5 of using a pencil to help you feel happy?

Respiratory etiquette

Coughing and sneezing without covering your mouth was never good behaviour, but now that its true harm is more widely known, unhindered coughing and sneezing have thankfully become a real social taboo. We can retrain ourselves to behave differently.

If you've not got a tissue, the crook of your bent elbow will stop coughs and sneezes blasting into the atmosphere – but you're reading this because you're survival-minded, so you will have prepared for this and have some tissues, right? Afterwards you need to clean your hands. This hand-cleaning advice holds for other times you may have touched a surface that could have droplets on it too; if you've successfully avoided inhaling droplets by social distancing, it would be a pity to then touch your eyes, nose or mouth if they've transferred onto your hands by contact, and let the virus in that way. If you know you have to enter a higher-risk zone like a public toilet or the petrol station (handling the pumps is something that you may not have already thought about), you can further protect yourself by using one of your tissues as a disposable barrier when you have to touch handles, etc.

Hand hygiene

When your hands are visibly dirty the best way to clean them is by washing with soap and water. Normal soap, the 'yardstick of civilization', works by helping the water to remove the particles from your hands, not by killing the germs that are now hiding out in the natural oils on your skin. Soap molecules work by making the oil particles (now containing pathogens) bond with water so they will rinse off together. Think of soap like loads of tiny chemical magnets, one end sticking to oil and the other end sticking to water, forcing two things that would normally not join up to bond together.[53] Soap is very good at its job of distancing you from potentially harmful microorganisms, but mechanically removing them by soap handwashing takes time, and that's why you need to be thorough. The WHO recommends you spend 40 to 60 seconds doing it.[54]

Alcohol-based hand gels can't cut through lots of muck and grease, which is why soap and water is better if your hands look dirty. However, even if they look clean, your hands will still have huge numbers of tiny organisms on them, some of which could be the COVID-19 virus. Alcohol is a solvent for your natural skin oils that the germs are sticking to, and works slightly differently. When the concentration of alcohol in hand gels is over 60 per cent,[55] there is enough alcohol for it to also destroy the outer protein shell of the virus, which will kill it. This takes a little less time than washing with soap: the WHO recommends hand gels be rubbed on your hands for 20 to 30 seconds.[56] Make sure you apply enough in the first place too; it should say how much on the label. And do always check the label: you need to know that there is at least a 60 per cent alcohol content, otherwise it's not going to kill the virus.

This link leads to a video of a World Health Organization doctor showing you the best way to get your hands clean (www.youtube.com/watch?v=y7e8nM0JAz0)

How to avoid touching your face

It's really hard to retrain yourself not to touch your own face. In the past, I've seen jungle survival instructors with machetes in their hands instinctively swat at mosquitoes. Even when you are trying not to touch your face, it happens before your conscious brain can override it, as we discussed in Chapter 1 when we looked at your brain's prehistoric, pre-programmed shortcuts. But, as we also saw there, we can reprogram our brains to react differently, to override our instinctive reactions through a process of practice drills.

Other than when we scratch itches, we touch our faces for a variety of reasons – studies have shown them to include 'self-soothing' and that skin-to-skin contact can release a hormone called oxytocin, which increases a feeling of calm – and if we're mindful of those reasons, we can intercept our hands en route to our faces. More practically, if you know you have a habit of touching your eyes, perhaps when you're tired, wear sunglasses. If you know you stroke your beard when you think, you could sit on your hands or put them in your pockets. If you need to scratch an itch, try using the back of your arm instead of your hands. As we covered in the detail about pilot emergency drills in Chapter 1, this is retraining your behaviours to have a specific, appropriate response, and is far more effective than just being told, 'don't do that unconscious thing that you do'.[57] But all these hacks take time to embed, and you'll never fully eliminate the chance of an unguarded moment, so keep washing your hands!

A good way to stop your hands physically touching your mouth and nose is to wear a face mask. It is being recommended that in situations where you are near other people, masks should be worn.

The best protection

Shelter-in-place. That's right, in your place. Remember, you could have the virus but not yet have the symptoms. Anyone who goes out to 'agglomerations' unnecessarily can pass the virus to two or three others, who can in turn spread it to two or three others, and repeat, until the healthcare system collapses, and vulnerable people die who could've lived. By simply staying at home, never can so many do so much for the few.

Coping with indefinite isolation

The most effective action we can take is to be responsible and stay at home. But it does not come without challenges because, aside from being social creatures, our species doesn't like uncertainty. Researchers at University College London proved this by measuring the sweat and pupil size of people playing a game where the prize for finding a snake behind a rock was a small electric shock. What they discovered in their study was that we are more stressed if we are uncertain whether a shock is coming than we are if we know we are going to get zapped.[58]

As we saw with stealth fighter pilot Dale Zelko in Chapter 1, you need to create a 'what if?' strategy to make coping with the unexpected easier – expect to be zapped. Doing this can't provide you with all the answers, but it can retrain your brain to avoid being overwhelmed by the unexpected, and to think more clearly when some new challenge presents itself. You can further reduce your stress by limiting the amount of time that you spend scrolling for 'news' through bottomless social media feeds. If you want to know concrete facts rather than vested opinions, go to the information sources like health officials and disease prevention agencies. It would be advisable to limit yourself to one or two news reports per day, rather than updates rolling on indefinitely on a screen. As we saw in my chapter on evasion, social media – and even rolling news programmes – are all designed to be extremely addictive.

We should reframe the situation psychologically, not by continuously monitoring our shelter-in-place screens and windows for threats, but by seizing the time it gives us as an opportunity to be usefully creative – Shakespeare supposedly wrote *King Lear* during the bubonic plague 'lockdown'. This is, hopefully, a once-in-a-lifetime opportunity to spend some uninterrupted time trying something new, so just get started and see what you can achieve. Far better to look back on the first draft of your novel when the pandemic has passed than wonder why you chose to watch every series on Netflix.

There are some groups who are experts in these isolation scenarios, from whom we can learn some useful tactics. Before automation, lighthouse keepers used to work in a team of three, each taking their turn 'on watch' – stints of time spent alone monitoring the light and fighting off sleep. The way they would start each period of duty would be by having a half-hour chat with the keeper going off watch. The off-going keeper really wanted to get their head on a pillow and sleep, but they knew they also had a responsibility to help their colleague who'd just got out of bed to become alert, so they would brew them a big pot of tea and share it over a natter.[59] If you know of any vulnerable friends or relatives who are stuck home alone, be a 'lightkeeper' and give them a call. And, if you can, a video call will let you actually see them and read their gestures; not only will they feel more connected but you get to keep an eye out for them and make sure they aren't struggling to cope.

When off watch and not sleeping, all lighthouse keepers had a hobby. You don't want to kill time during this unexpected window of opportunity, you want to spend it well. What's a good hobby to choose? Reading is one of the best ways to reduce stress. It was found to be 68 per cent better at reducing stress levels than listening to music, 300 per cent better than going for a walk and 700 per cent more than playing video games.[60] And if you choose some nonfiction books to read, it could be that you learn something new too. If reading isn't what your family are into, podcasts can be a brilliant way to dial into the conversations of interesting and inspirational people. Online learning courses are also a great use of this gift of time; many are available with audio feeds if you want to limit screen or sitting hours. You could also make things with your hands, like finishing that DIY task that you've not had time to do before, or something with a more tangible reward like setting up some home brew.

Looking at best practices from which we can learn how to cope better with isolation, another group who are very well adapted to not being able to nip out for a coffee are the astronauts of the International Space Station. Long periods in close proximity to others is not just about being with the right people, it's about being the right person yourself. As Canadian astronaut Chris Hadfield says, 'These days, NASA looks for a certain type of person, someone who plays well with others.'[61] Interestingly, Chris thinks he gained a lot of insight into teamwork and 'playing well with others' during his survival training.[62] When you are dependent on the few people around you and your joint initiative, success really is a team sport. Establishing a routine where any unpleasant tasks are shared equally, and some time is dedicated to personal space, will help this. And as we saw in Chapter 5 where we looked at the importance of other people in survival, remaining good-humoured is a massive asset, and directly in your power to control.

Think of the current situation you are in as your own survival training: it can be tough in the moment, but afterwards I reckon we will look back and appreciate the lessons we have learned. When I come back from the Arctic, I always enjoy the spring sunshine more than I used to; when home from the jungle, it's great not to have to check for leeches before bed. After this pandemic, I know I'll really appreciate the regained freedom to mooch to the pub, and we're all less likely to take life's simple pleasures for granted.

By following these simple guidelines, you'll have a PLAN ready for any enforced period of self-isolation in the future. Added to which, you won't become collateral damage in any uncool fight over toilet paper.

To panic or to prepare

Toilet paper panic-buying is the perfect metaphor for the combination of unhelpful rumour and inappropriate behaviour. Normal society runs on good behaviour, but it only needs one selfish person to take more than they need 'just in case' and a domino effect of panic-buying ensues, to the point where people are mass-buying anything they can get their hands on, not even *knowing why* they needed so much toilet paper. What is slightly comic to watch at first very quickly leads to serious consequences, when it leaves healthcare workers coming off eye-reddeningly long shifts to find that they can't even buy fruit and vegetables and the kind of food that they, more than anyone, need to stay healthy. Call it what you like – panic-buying, FOMO, the tragedy of the commons – it's antisocial, selfish and wrong. We are in this together.

There is no *need* for people to behave like we're an idiocracy; we can choose how we respond to any challenge.

If you witness selfish types overstocking, the traditional British response – and denouncement of all socially unacceptable conduct – is a well-aimed 'tut'. But, given these exceptional circumstances, and knowing that this behaviour has already impacted hard-pressed emergency services and healthcare professionals, why not really signify how inappropriate panic-buying is as a community response and ask the pusher of the overloaded trolley if they really need that much toilet paper? If everyone takes a stance, it should put the shelves back in balance for all. Again, it's about being polite, confident and taking individual responsibility for the whole team.

So how can you avoid being affected by that kind of reactionary nonsense in the future? In the short term, your local shops and smaller stores might still have what you need – bigger superstores seem to get stripped out first. And if it's available where you live, online shopping is a great alternative in these conditions. In the longer term, once all the dust from COVID-19 settles, you'll want a PLAN to weather any future social 'storms'. Unless you're 'prepping' for doomsday,* the sequence and stats from Chapter 2 about what your body actually requires hold true: 'To summarize and generalize: if you can't breathe or are bleeding heavily, time to death is in **minutes**, uninjured at extremes of temperature it's in **hours**, without any drinking water death takes **days**, and without food, **weeks**.'

* Google TEOTWAWKI if you're curious.

So there really is no need to bury a container with a tonne of rice and grenades in the woods.

Remember that things like a good first-aid kit are top of your list, then ways to protect yourself physically – including perhaps a face mask or two – to maintain your body temperature, and importantly to stay informed. Many people don't know that batteries to power radios and torches will have a use-by date, so check them every so often – a good routine is whenever you change the clocks in spring or autumn. You will need clean drinking water more than food, so have a couple of options to make your own as the next event could see people panic-buying bottled water too: boiling water is the best way, but purification tablets can be bought online, are cheap and take up hardly any space. If you aren't one of the few who can harvest what they need to eat from the great outdoors all year round, then get some unperishable food that won't attract pests. How much you store is up to you, but you shouldn't need a huge amount, and no more than thirty days' worth based on minimal activity. Again, you'll need to keep an eye on use-by dates, so write these on the tops of cans and packets in bold before you store them under your stairs to make that task easier. Knowing you have these things set aside reduces the mental pressure of seeing people panic-buy on the news.

If you do find yourself making odd or impulsive decisions, it may be a sign that you need to rebalance yourself and regain some perspective. As we saw at the beginning of the book, a well-stocked and well-functioning brain is the best survival tool anyone can have.

What now?

How we deal with adversity defines us. If you're feeling more stressed than usual, that is understandable in these unprecedented, uncertain times. But everything can be dealt with, with the right mindset and techniques. If you feel overwhelmed, breathe – the breathing technique in Chapter 1 will help.

And as we saw with the amazing escape of the three Aussie aircrew in Chapter 4, breaking any task down into smaller, achievable chunks is the key to maintaining hope. Hope allows you to plan for the future, which in turn gets you started in tackling the issue and also spins up a positive feedback loop: your own engine of perseverance.

We can learn from the Stoic philosophy of Jim Stockdale, who spent over seven years in the 'Hanoi Hilton' prison during the Vietnam War after his jet was shot down: mentally dividing things into those you can control and those that you can't control will reduce your worries. He knew the works of ancient philosophers like Epictetus by heart and he endured unimaginable hardship in actual physical and mental isolation by employing their core ideas daily, hourly. At the heart of survival of any situation, from the most mundane to extreme, from the known to the completely novel like the current pandemic, the key is to think like a Stoic: to accept the circumstances, understand the controllable and the uncontrollable and the difference between the two, and adapt your mindset accordingly. Humankind has been presented with challenges for as long as civilization has existed and Epictetus got it right when he talked about the Stoic's mindset nearly 2,000 years ago.

And remember, you have been gifted some time at home – I hope just the simple act of reading this has reduced your stress and given you some ideas and motivation; the conditions are ripe to gain new knowledge and skills for the future.

Good luck.

APPENDIX 2
HOW TO LIGHT A FIRE

One of the key elements in survival training that transcends all of the facets of PLAN is firelighting. When you master this, you can brew-up almost anywhere, and it's not as difficult to learn as you might think. As we've seen earlier, to really gain knowledge takes a combination of semantic and episodic memories, so read this then practise! You will need a few items of kit to make this happen easily, and it goes without saying that fires are not to be lit in the wrong places, at the wrong times of year.* Always choose bare ground, away from plants and trees and anything else that sparks could spread onto. The best place to practise outside to begin with is in an empty barbecue that is designed to have a fire in it and that won't leave a fire scar afterwards.

---

* Never light fires outdoors when there's been a long spell of dry weather, or on very dry ground. Fires can spread very quickly and cause huge damage.

The vital components of all fires are heat, fuel and oxygen – think of them as a tripod that has to be able to stand up, meaning you have to find the right balance of the three components. You can most easily strike this balance with a fire kit of matches, cotton wool balls, a small pocket-knife like a Victorinox Hiker, and a small bag of kindling wood, like the ones they sell at garage forecourts. And don't forget the magic ingredient; a ChapStick, any flavour. With this little collection you have enough good stuff to practise lighting several fires, and the repetition will help to really embed the knowledge. Here's what to do, step by step.

Step 1 - Preparation

Getting a fire to light is a bit like accelerating a car; you turn its ignition and then go through the gears until everything is running at cruising speed. Firelighting is all about preparation of your materials, so do that first before you go near the ignition sequence. Also, you can't go for too high a gear too soon, it would stall. So you need to have your kindling graded – the bits you pull out of the kindling bag are the biggest bits you'll have, and should only be used to hit top gear. The most time-consuming part of preparation is making some bits of kindling smaller – to burn at lower gears – by splitting them down into thinner pieces.

When you start using your knife, get into good habits

early. Always cut away from yourself, and keep your fleshy bits behind the cutting edge at all times, never in front of it. Don't cut down onto stone, earth or metal as they will hurt your blade; cut onto a wooden surface – a vegetable chopping board will do to start with. Get used to your knife by initially just shaving small slithers from down the corner edges of some kindling wood, always going with the grain. If you see any pieces of wood with knots in them, don't bother trying to cut them as the knots will jam your blade – save those bits for burning whole. By the time you've practised shaving the corners off a few straight-grained knot-free pieces, you should have a small pile of wood shavings, hopefully none of them stained with drops of red. Keep those shavings; they are first gear. It's always good to have more than you think you'll need, so make sure the pile is as big as four of your other sticks.

Step 2 - Preparation

The next stage of prep is to split some straight-grained, knot-free pieces of kindling lengthways. To do this, stand the piece of kindling vertically on the chopping board and gently place your knife's cutting edge on the top. Never leave your other hand below the blade – if the piece you've chosen doesn't stand up without your non-cutting hand holding it, swap it for one that will. You're going to split this piece by tapping the knife's blade gently downwards, using another, bigger bit of wood as a mallet. This way all your digits are behind the cutting edge and the whole job is stable and controlled. Tap firmly only on the back of the knife's blade, not any hinge or folding joint, as that could damage your knife. What you will end up with is the bit of straight-grained kindling popping apart into two thinner bits as the blade slowly taps down its length. You can now repeat this process on one half of the split stick to make a quarter-sized piece. The combination of shavings, quarter-width, half-width and full-size kindling are the gears you need to accelerate your fire to burning speed. You just need more of them now, so get splitting until you think you have plenty, then double it.

Step 3 - Preparation

That's the main fuel prepared, now here's how to get ready for actually lighting your fire. All survival fires need to be clear of the cold, damp ground, so the first thing to prepare is a base; it's going to protect the young fire and allow air to circulate in it, adding that vital ingredient from the fire triangle – oxygen. The base is easy to make; simply lay four bits of full-sized kindling down on your barbecue, right next to each other like the closed fingers on a wooden hand. Now we'll start to arrange the ingredients. To make sure that you don't smother your fire, put one more piece of kindling wood down on top of the base you've just made, but at a right angle to the other four bits, and place it right to the end of those pieces, across their imaginary wooden fingernails. The remaining, uncovered part of the base 'fingers' is where we are going to ignite the fire. The 'fingernail' piece is more properly known as the backboard, and you'll be able to lean smaller pieces against it, over the small flame to come, without dropping them directly on the flame and smothering it accidentally.

Step 4 - Preparation

Now take a cotton wool ball, making sure to keep it dry, and squash a half-centimetre piece of the magic ingredient – the ChapStick – into it. Next, tease some of the shape back into the ball so that it's not too compacted. The petroleum jelly in the ChapStick will act like the wax does in a candle – making the cotton ball burn for a longer time while your fire gets going. Place this next to the centre of the backboard on your fire base.

Before you reach for the matches, here's what you'll do *after* ignition. It's better to know this in advance! Have all the fuel that you prepared earlier laid out next to you in easy reach, and graded from small to big. Once the cotton wool is lit, you'll add the smallest shavings five or six at a time by gently placing a small handful of them across the flame, so that their ends rest on the backboard. The backboard will raise them at one end and that angle will stop them from cutting off the oxygen supply to the flame. When the first few are on, lay the next few at 90 degrees over the top of them, in a criss-cross pattern. Keep doing this at a nice steady pace; if you go too slow they'll burn out before igniting the next ones, too quick and you'll smother the flame. This is where your practise makes perfect; you build episodic memories of 'how to' by doing. Once the pile of shavings is used up, go to your quarter-width pieces and lay them on in the same way. Then half-width and finally full-sized kindling sticks.

Step 5 – Ignition

Now and only now, after all this preparation, is it time to strike a match and light the cotton wool and ChapStick ball. There's actually a right way to strike a match, but we'll cover that another time. Good luck, and don't worry if it isn't easy first time; it will be after several goes.

Being able to light a fire is something that our ancestors would've known how to do as intimately as we understand googling. As well as enabling you to make a brew and dry your socks, fire has an application within every single part of the survival PLAN. Once you have practised using your fire kit, you can get more ambitious, finding more of the fuel to use while actually on your hike or using a spark rather than a match to ignite the cotton wool. Eventually you'll replace cotton wool with birch bark or lichens, and be setting out with just your knife, fire-steel and metal mug to brew up. With a little more experience, you'll be able to go for long trips with just what's in your pockets.

APPENDIX 3
HOW TO BUILD AN IGLOO

You need the right kind of snow to build an igloo, and you have to choose it carefully as conditions can vary within the space of a couple of metres. That's why the Inuit famously have many different words to describe types of snow, the general term being 'anniu'. I've been lucky enough to learn more skills of the far north by working closely with the Inuit Rangers and the Canadian SERE team over two winters, first as a student and then, on my second trip, I was honoured to be invited back as an instructor.

First, you have to find a good patch of packed-down snow – 'pukajaw' – that makes the squeaky polystyrene noise when you walk on it. It needs to be hard enough to not let your feet sink in as you walk over it – they call that looser stuff 'ariloqaq' – but not so hard that it can't be cut with a snow knife or saw – this 'sitijucuaw' snow can be as hard as stone.

To cut the snow, the tools used are just modern versions of ones that were originally made from whale or caribou bone. A simple flat blade, around a foot long, was formed from a rib bone and given a cutting edge made of ice; water was squirted from the mouth of the knife wielder onto its blade and then it was sharpened. The modern ones are long metal 'snow knives', simple but effective, with large angled handles that are easy to grip with thick mittens. On an Arctic survival course, it's common to see students probing the snow with these knives as they walk, hunting for the right 'pukajaw' conditions to build with.

If the snow has the right consistency all the way down the blade, then cut the blocks out vertically like slices of bread from a loaf, called the 'crack way' by the locals. If, as sometimes happens, the conditions haven't been perfect and only a thin layer is suitable, you'll have to cut them out like paving stones – the 'open way' – which takes much longer,. The Inuit are an infinitely adaptable people, and the more time I spend up there, learning their ingenious solutions to extreme cold-weather living, the more I appreciate their impressive ability to adapt what little resources they have.

As soon as you start working, even if it's -30°C or below, you warm up dramatically. The amount of heat that your body generates as it works is impressive too, up to 1500W, equivalent to the output of a small domestic electric heater. This means it's vital to remove some warm layers of clothing as you start to work. If you don't, you'll sweat. If you sweat, the clothing gets wet. Wet clothing kills quickly in the Arctic because the wetness becomes ice inside the garment and conducts your body heat away as soon as you stop working. It's hard to tell if you're sweating too, so take off some warm layers and open some fasteners to vent until it feels chilly, and then work slowly but steadily. Or you will die. Sweat kills – it is that brutal up there.

Once you've cut enough snow blocks out, start to build a circular wall that is constructed to slope inwards slightly. Trim every block with the knife as it's placed in position to ensure a snug fit. Because the friction from this trimming also warms the block's edge up slightly, each new block sticks to the adjoining blocks as its edges cool back down.

The secret of an igloo is its spiral design. Trim the tops of three blocks from your first layer to make a gentle wedge or ramp that will start the spiral. To make building easier, right-handed people coil their igloos anti-clockwise, left-handed people will work clockwise. Then add blocks, starting from the bottom of the ramp, with each new block touching the last and overlapping the joints of those below. Secure each block by tapping down firmly, angled with the same slight inwards lean as before. Provided each block has three points of contact with the others below and next to it, and the gradual lean is maintained, a gravity-defying dome emerges from the snowfield. The 'quarry' hole in the snowfield's surface from which the blocks were cut will extend a short way inside the igloo, creating a 'cold well' at the doorway; cold air sinks and having your sleeping area higher than the door top ensures you'll be warm inside. The igloo is the pinnacle of shelter ingenuity and means that those who know how to build one need only carry a snow knife in order to have a home.

ACKNOWLEDGEMENTS

The idea for this book started to come alive over five years ago when I sat down for a brew in London with Jo Cantello and Jamie Coleman. If it wasn't for their continued support and guidance as agent and editor over the intervening teas that became years, this project couldn't have happened (and it certainly wouldn't look the way it does as you read it now) without their ever-constructive feedback. Thanks to you and your respective teams of ever-helpful and insightful professionals.

Once Jo and Jamie had started our creative conversations that helped me to design the book, I depended on the knowledge that was generously shared by the many local experts with whom it's been my privilege to work over the last twenty years. They range from my Iban friends in Borneo to the Inuit of the high Arctic, and include all the many military instructors of the Allied nations I've trained with in between. Special thanks to the team at the Canadian Forces school in Winnipeg and Dave Dawson from the Australian Forces survival school for their time and forbearance.

John Leach and Dale Zelko were both generous and patient with their correspondence, and in their assistance in providing source material, feedback and insight; thank you for fitting the keystone in my understanding of the psychology arch.

My friends and mentors Dave, Matt, Alf and Tony all willingly subjected themselves to reading early chapter drafts and then took the time to donate ideas of improvements. There were lots. Thank you all.

All projects get built upon foundations, and this one wouldn't have been possible without the help and understanding from my wife Jen. Thank you for enthusiastically supporting me as I tapped away all of our spare time at the laptop, and drove you the length and breadth of this island in the name of research.

And thank you to all the staff and students, past and present, of the UK military survival school, from whom I've never stopped learning.

NOTES

1   Littlewood, Tom and Dabrowska, Barbara (trans.) (2011) 'After the fall': https://harpers.org/archive/2011/01/after-the-fall/

2   Leach, John (1994) *Survival Psychology* (London: Palgrave Macmillan), p. 10.

3   Ibid., p. 30.

4   Ibid., pp. 23–5.

5   Robinson, S., Bridges, N., Leach, J. and Sheals, K. (2012) 'An Investigation into the Effects of Chewing Gum Containing Caffeine and L-theanine on Cognitive Processing and Stress Responses After a Strenuous Fire-Fighting Exercise'. BPS Psychobiology Conference, Windermere.

6   Wong, Sam (2017) 'How to train your brain to be like a memory champion's'. Available at: https://www.newscientist.com/article/2123945-how-to-train-your-brain-to-be-like-a-memory-champions/

7   National Museum of the United States Airforce, Wings & Things Guest Lecture Series, 'The Unthinkable, the Unimaginable Happened: An F-117 was Shot Down in Combat'. Available at: https://www.nationalmuseum.af.mil/Portals/7/documents/transcripts/f117_shot_down_transcript.pdf

8   Baddeley, A. and Godden, D. (1975) 'Context-Dependent Memory in Two Natural Environments: On Land and Underwater', *British Journal of Psychology* [online], 66 (3),

pp. 325–31. Available at: https://msu.edu/course/psy/401/ Readings/Godden%20&%20Baddeley%20(1975).pdf

9   Cuddy, Amy (2016) *Presence* (London: Orion), p. 224.

10 See, for example: Gilbert, D. (2006) *Stumbling on Happiness* (London: Harper Press); Douglas, Kate (2011) 'Decision time: How subtle forces shape your choices'. Available at: https://www.newscientist .com/article/mg21228381-800-decision-time-how-subtle-forces-shape-your-choices/

11 See Tracy, Brian (2013) *Eat That Frog!* (London: Hodder).

12 Duckworth, Angela (2013) 'What is grit?' interview with John Templeton Foundation, available at: https://www.youtube .com/watch?v=Rkoe1e2KZJs&t=12s.

13 Statler, T. and Kress, J. (2007) 'A naturalistic investigation of former Olympic cyclists' cognitive strategies for coping with exertion pain during performance', *Journal of Sport Behaviour* [online], 30 (4), pp. 428–52. Available at: http://sirc.ca/sites/ default/files/content/docs/newsletters/archive/July12/ documents/Free/Fighting%20Through%20Pain.pdf [accessed 27 August 2016].

14 Alter, Adam (2017) *Irresistible* (London: Vintage), p. 69.

15 Mark, Gloria, Gudith, Daniela and Klocke, Ulrich (2008) 'The cost of interrupted work: More speed and stress', Proceedings of the SIGCHI Conference on Human Factors in Computing Systems (CHI '08). ACM, New York, 107–110. DOI: 10.1145/ 1357054.1357072.

16 NHS, 'Why we should sit less': https://www.nhs.uk/live-well/ exercise/why-sitting-too-much-is-bad-for-us/

17 Duckworth, Angela (2016) *Grit* (London: Penguin), p. 144.

18 Quoted from the log of the *Anglo Saxon*'s jolly boat, viewed by the author at the Imperial War Museum, London.

19 Allport, G., Lasch, I. and Frankl, V. (2004) *Man's Search for Meaning: The classic tribute to hope from the Holocaust* (Croydon: Rider & Co.), p. 80.

20 Seligman, M. E. P. (2006) *Learned Optimism: How to change your mind and your life* (New York: Vintage Books), p. 28.

21 Booth, George (1988) *33 Days: A Story of Courage and Endurance* (Elwood: Greenhouse), p. 23.

22 Stockdale, J. (2001) 'Stockdale on Stoicism II: Master of my Fate', US Naval Academy, Center for the Study of Professional Military Ethics. Available at: https://www.usna.edu/Ethics/_files/documents/Stoicism2.pdf [accessed 28 August 2016].

23 Maslow, A. (1943) 'A Theory of Human Motivation', *Psychological Review*, 50 (4), pp. 370–96.

24 Seligman, *Learned Optimism*, p. 174.

25 Jones, E. E. and Harris, V. A. (1967) 'The attribution of attitudes', *Journal of Experimental Social Psychology*, 3 (1), pp. 1–24. Available at: https://www.radford.edu/~jaspelme/443/spring-2007/Articles/Jones_n_Harris_1967.pdf

26 Galinsky, A. and Adam, H. (2012) 'Enclothed cognition', *Journal of Experimental Social Psychology* [online], 48 (4), pp. 918–25. Available at: http://www.sciencedirect.com/science/article/pii/S0022103112000200 [accessed 7 November 2016].

27 Fernandes, M., Meade, M. and Wammes, J. (2016) 'The drawing effect: Evidence for reliable and robust memory benefits in free recall', *Quarterly Journal of Experimental Psychology* 69 (9), pp. 1752–76.

28 A term popularized by the psychologist Carol Dweck, but the phenomenon had been discussed anecdotally for years by survival instructors.

29 Christakis, N., Nowak, M., Rand, D. and Hill, A. (2010) 'Emotions as infectious diseases in a large social network: The SISa model', *Proceedings of the Royal Society B: Biological Sciences* [online], 277 (1701), pp. 3827–35. Available at: http://rspb.royalsociety publishing.org/content/royprsb/277/1701/3827.full.pdf [accessed 29 August 2016].

30 Sy, T., Cote, S. and Saavedra, R. (2005) 'The Contagious Leader: Impact of the Leader's Mood on the Mood of Group Members, Group Affective Tone, and Group Processes', *Journal of Applied Psychology*, 90 (2), 295–305. Available at: https://pdfs.semanticscholar.org/d9bf/af51cf9894657b814adfb342ff2 5948877e0.pdf [accessed 29 August 2016].

31 Strack, F., Martin, L. L. and Stepper, S. (1988) 'Inhibiting and facilitating conditions of the human smile: A nonobtrusive test of the facial feedback hypothesis', *Journal of Personality and Social Psychology*, 54 (5), 768–77.

32 Sinek, Simon (2011) *Start With Why* (London: Penguin), p. 138.

33 Franklin said this to the last ship to see them alive in Baffin Bay. See Atwood, M., Geiger, J. and Beattie, O. (2005) *Frozen in Time: The fate of the Franklin expedition* (3rd edn.) (Vancouver: Douglas & McIntyre Publishing Group), p. 45.

34 McGoogan, Ken and Rae, John (2012) *The Arctic Journals of John Rae* (Canada: Touchwood), p. 33.

35 Bagnold, R. and Bagnold, S. (2012) *Libyan Sands* (London: Eland Publishing), p. 20.

36 As quoted in Dobbs, David (2013) 'Restless Genes'. Available at: https://www.nationalgeographic.com/magazine/2013/01/restless-genes/

37 Kardan, O. (2015) 'Neighborhood greenspace and health in a large urban center', *Nature Scientific Reports* [online] 5 (11610). Available at: http://www.nature.com/articles/srep11610 [accessed 9 November 2016].

38 Vyssoki, B., Kapusta, N. D., Praschak-Rieder, N., Dorffner, G. and Willeit, M. (2014) 'Direct Effect of Sunshine on Suicide', *JAMA Psychiatry*, 71 (11): 1231–7. DOI: 10.1001/jamapsychiatry.2014.1198

39 Jefferies, Richard (2002) *The Story of My Heart: My Autobiography* (Cambridge: Green Books), p. 3.

40 See, for example: Alter, *Irresistible*, p. 220.

41 Chapman, F. (1949) *The Jungle is Neutral* (London: Chatto & Windus), p. 118.

42 Ibid., p. 177.

43 As quoted in Stockdale, J. (2001) 'Stockdale on Stoicism II: Master of My Fate', US Naval Academy, Center for the Study of Professional Military Ethics. Available at: https://www.usna.edu/Ethics/_files/documents/Stoicism2.pdf

44 Scientific American (2004) 'Are viruses alive?': https://www.scientificamerican.com/article/are-viruses-alive-2004/

45 New Scientist (2020) 'We're beginning to understand the biology of the COVID-19 virus': https://www.newscientist.com/article/mg24532743-500-were-beginning-to-understand-the-biology-of-the-covid-19-virus/
46 World Health Organization, 'Coronavirus': https://www.who.int/health-topics/coronavirus
47 New Scientist (2020) 'Wuhan coronavirus may have been transmitted to people from snakes': https://www.newscientist.com/article/2231162-wuhan-coronavirus-may-have-been-transmitted-to-people-from-snakes/
48 CNN, 'Infected people without symptoms might be driving the spread of coronavirus more than we realized': https://edition.cnn.com/2020/03/14/health/coronavirus-asymptomatic-spread/index.html
49 World Health Organization, OpenWHO online course, 'Emerging respiratory viruses, including COVID-19: methods for detection, prevention, response and control': https://openwho.org/courses/introduction-to-ncov
50 New Scientist (2020) 'We're beginning to understand the biology of the covid-19 virus'
51 World Health Organization, OpenWHO online course, 'Emerging respiratory viruses, including COVID-19: methods for detection, prevention, response and control'
52 World Health Organization, OpenWHO online course, 'ePROTECT Respiratory Infections, Module 2: How to protect yourself against Acute Respiratory Infections (ARIs)': https://openwho.org/courses/eprotect-acute-respiratory-infections/
53 Scientific American (2016) 'Does Soap Really Kill 99.9 Percent of Germs?': https://www.scientificamerican.com/article/does-soap-really-kill-99-9-percent-of-germs/
54 World Health Organization, OpenWHO online course, 'ePROTECT Respiratory Infections, Module 3: Basic hygiene measures': https://openwho.org/courses/eprotect-acute-respiratory-infections/
55 Center for Disease Control and Prevention, 'Chemical Disinfectants': https://www.cdc.gov/infectioncontrol/guidelines/disinfection/disinfection-methods/chemical.html
56 World Health Organization, OpenWHO online course, 'ePROTECT Respiratory Infections, Module 3: Basic hygiene measures'.

57 Michael Hallsworth, behavioural scientist at Columbia University, via BBC, 'How to avoid touching your face so much.'

58 de Berker, A., Rutledge, R., Mathys, C. et al. 'Computations of uncertainty mediate acute stress responses in humans'. *Nat Commun* 7, 10996 (2016). DOI: 10.1038/ncomms10996

59 Hill, P. (2004) *Stargazing: Memoirs of a Young Lighthouse Keeper* (Canongate), p. 92.

60 The Reading Agency, 'Reading Well evidence base': https://readingagency.org.uk/adults/impact/research/reading-well-books-on-prescription-scheme-evidence-base.html.

61 Hadfield, C. (2013) *An Astronaut's Guide to Life on Earth* (Macmillan), p.103.

62 Ibid, p. 104.